The Nature of Economic Thought

ADVANCES IN ECONOMIC METHODOLOGY

General Editor: Warren J. Samuels
Michigan State University, US

This major new series presents original and innovative work in economic methodology, including all aspects of the philosophy, sociology and rhetoric of economics as well as the relationship of economics to other disciplines.

The series reflects the renewed interest in all aspects of economic methodology as well as the deepening sense both of conceptual and technical crisis plaguing the economics profession and that the crisis involves deep methodological considerations. It is also hoped that the series will contribute to the better understanding and solution of the economic problems of both mature and developing countries.

The series is open to all points of view and approaches.

Truth versus Precision in Economics
Thomas Mayer

John Maynard Keynes
Language and Method
Edited by Alessandra Marzola and Francesco Silva

Classical Economic Man
Human Agency and Methodology in the Political Economy
of Adam Smith and J.S. Mill
Allen Oakley

The Nature of Economic Thought
Essays in Economic Methodology
Johannes J. Klant

The Nature of Economic Thought

Essays in Economic Methodology

Johannes J. Klant

Professor Emeritus of Economics, University of Amsterdam

Translated by
Trevor S. Preston

Edward Elgar

© Johannes J. Klant 1994

Published by
Edward Elgar Publishing Limited
Gower House
Croft Road
Aldershot
Hants GU11 3HR
England

Edward Elgar Publishing Company
Old Post Road
Brookfield
Vermont 05036
USA

British Library Cataloguing in Publication Data
Klant, Johannes J.
    Nature of Economic Thought: Essays in
    Economic Methodology.–(Advances in
    Economic Methodology)
    I. Title II. Series
    330.01

Library of Congress Cataloguing in Publication Data
Klant, J. J.
    The nature of economic thought: essays in economic methodology/
Johannes J. Klant: translated by Trevor S. Preston. — [1st ed.]
        p.   cm. — (Advances in economic methodology)
    Revised, adapted and partly translated essays.
    Includes bibliographical references and index.
    1. Economics—Methodology.   I. Title.   II. Series.
HB131.K58   1994
330'.01—dc20   93–38551
                                                                CIP

ISBN 1 85898 018 6

Printed and bound in Great Britain by
Hartnolls Limited, Bodmin, Cornwall

Contents

Figures

Preface

In this volume eight chapters have been assembled which all centre on an idea about the logical structure of economic thought. Each chapter has been separately published before. For the purpose of this volume they have been revised and adapted.

Part I (Chapters 1–4) is the translation of a booklet published in the Netherlands on the philosophy of economic thought which was written for economists as well for non-economists (for example, philosophers). This explains why some matters have been expounded in a very simplified way.

Chapter 5 was published as a series of short articles in *Methodus* (vol. 2, nos 2, 3 and 4), the third article of which has been completely rewritten.

Chapter 6 was published in the now discontinued journal *Methodology and Science* (VII – 1974).

The two remaining chapters were papers submitted to two conferences and have been published in:

Lawson, T. and Pesaran, H. (eds), *Keynes' Economics*. London: Routledge, 1989.
De Marchi, N. (ed.), *The Popperian Legacy in Economics*, Cambridge: Cambridge University Press, 1988.

They are reprinted here by kind permission of Routledge and Cambridge University Press.

Part I and chapter 8 have been translated from Klant's original Dutch by Trevor S. Preston. Chapters 5, 6 and 7 were written by the author in English.

PART I
The Nature of Economic Thought

1. From Political Economy to Economics

LOOKING ON AND TAKING PART

According to Plato and Aristotle, wonder forms the beginning of knowledge. The 18th-century philosopher Adam Smith, who was one of the founding fathers of what today is called economics, proclaimed a philosophy of science in which, in emulation of the example of Antiquity, he regarded the successive and intensifying feelings of surprise, wonder and admiration as the incentives for research. Philosophers, as students of natural science, too, were called in his day, are driven by surprise and wonder at the riddles that present themselves to us (Smith [1795] 1980, pp. 33–47). This leads them to the discovery of *systems*, in which events are linked in accordance with the 'binding principles of nature' – which to Smith also includes society. They are, says Smith, like machines, the observation of which arouses joy. He was impressed by Descartes's and Newton's cosmology, and a machine was still a wonder. The natural order created by God appears to him 'in the philosophical light' as an immense and beautiful mechanism (Smith [1759] 1976a, p. 316).

The emotions of the philosophers that Smith describes are principally those of an onlooker at a relatively safe distance. He devoted little attention to a further instinctive involvement (in the world of man in particular) which sets the philosophers thinking: in addition to being lookers-on, we are, after all, participants. People are busy beings, constantly trying to achieve something, in co-operation or conflict, driven by need and ambition.

The participant who, in the midst of the hustle and bustle, observes human activity, is seized not only by wonder – which introduces curiosity – but also by concern at what we each do separately and bring about jointly. The participating lookers-on wish not only to understand the world in which they take part, have interests and run risks, but also to assess and change it. Action always means change, however slight.

Economic research emanates from a form of concerned attention that distinguishes it even from medical science. Economics is the child of ethics and politics. Economic research deals with what we ourselves make. It is a social science, a behavioural science and, because it relates to human creations, a cultural science. This also makes it a historical science; however, often economists try their best to ignore history.

Economic history began several hundred thousand years ago, when hominids made the first tools and then also learnt to master fire. Henceforth, production to meet our biocultural needs took place by labour with the aid of means of production made in advance. Economic growth is not an invention of economists or capitalists, but of an anthropoid ape.

The ingenuity of *Homo sapiens*, who by his cultural creativity conquered the Earth, attended thereafter to many more technical innovations. After an extremely slow start covering many thousands of years, the development of modern science rendered possible the considerable progress that has changed the world beyond recognition in the last three centuries.

Once upon a time, work – some 15 hours a week – must have been performed within small tribes of humans, as approximately today among the Bushmen. The tasks were divided among the members of the group according to age and sex. They shared with one another the products that they acquired by hunting and gathering (Sahlins, 1974). Later, procreation, amalgamation and violent subjection led to large, stratified communities; production came to be performed in separate households, between which division of labour and thus exchange of products came into being to an increasing extent.

The terms of exchange were established in the Neolithic from the above or by the participants in the transaction in accordance with a system of rights and duties that depended on power, status, function, age, prosperity, urgency of needs, family ties and kind of commodities; that is to say in accordance with prevailing views on what was *just*. To facilitate exchange, media of exchange became the vogue, which evolved into a special medium, namely coinage.

In the course of time the organization of production and distribution underwent changes, in each case accompanied by reinforcement of growth. The drastic changes in the European field of vision took place as a result of the Neolithic revolution, when long before our era the transition occurred to predominantly agricultural production; as a result of the commercial revolution of the Middle Ages, when the cities of Europe sprang up and the foundations were laid for capitalism; the agricultural revolution, which started in the 18th century, when as a result of the expanding capitalist agriculture the pronounced increase in agricultural productivity began that is still going on today; the industrial revolution, which since the end of the 18th century has led to an ever greater industrialization in an ever larger part of the world. Money dematerialized and became bank money, consisting of bank accounts and banknotes.

Some 2 500 years ago Athenian sophists taught administration (*nomeuein*) of the economy, both of the private household and of the city (*polis*). Aristotle calls that art *oikonomikè* or *politikè*. As *political economy*, *économie politique* and *Nationalökonomie* or *Volkswirtschaftslehre*, it continued to exist in Europe until the beginning of this century, when, as the result of scientific ambitions, the term *economics* became popular. The field concerns itself with economic problems in society – and hence also those proceeding from the activity of the State. Problems of the individual economic units are dealt with by *business economics*.

DECENCY, JUSTICE AND HEALTH

Plato and Aristotle, who lived through the decline of the Athenian commercial state, looked down with distaste on the money-earning and dealing around them. The desire to change the world is often directed towards a return to an idealized past. The *natural order*, the world as it ought to be, formed for them the 'good old days'. They cherished a Neolithic ideal. Plato proclaimed the end of economic growth – something that under alarming circumstances happens more than once. According to Aristotle the natural means of existence were farming, hunting, piracy and war. Trade and crafts were indecent. The interest demanded by money-lenders was also unnatural in his eyes, and was rightly hated.

Aristotle speaks of prices in his lessons on justice. In price-fixing, allowance must be made not only for the utility of the individual goods, but also for the inequality of the persons of the buyer and seller. The significance of this is rather obscure, but what Aristotle probably meant is that producers ought to be remunerated according to their standing in society. To him the inequality of people is based on differences in social status. The just price had to help to foster social equilibrium (Gordon, 1975, pp. 54–7).

The early Christians shared in their humility the aristocratic dislike of the Greek philosophers for trade, but under the impact of the commercial revolution the medieval philosophers (schoolmen) devised a natural order in which trade was permitted in moderation and at just prices. However, interest was forbidden among Christians. To Aristotle, barter had been an incidental transaction between two economic units that exchanged surplus goods to help one another. But the schoolmen had become familiar with the existence of markets in which large numbers of buyers and sellers met one another under the supervision of the authorities. The just price (*justum pretium*) was to them the 'natural price' that was the same for everyone and was formed on a well-functioning market by buyers and sellers.

A just price, in the opinion of the 16th-century Spanish theologian Luis de Molina, is the price that comes about in the market-place where all the citizens of the town have assembled. To 'come together' is, in Latin, *concurrere*. Concurrence brings about what was called in Roman law a *communis aestimatio*, a common estimation in the market-place. If the market does not work properly, for instance because of an insufficient number of suppliers or an abnormal shortage in the supply of goods, it is the task of the authorities to fix the just price, at least for the necessities of life (*pretium legitimum*). Profits in excess of normal profit, which recompense the merchant for his efforts on the market, are unacceptable.

The further development of political economy manifests itself in a changing interpretation of what was once designated *communis aestimatio*. According to medieval man, market prices are based on a common judgement, which is just. That evaluation was later to be regarded as a regulating rational principle, which is not necessarily just, but desirable, because it is 'natural'. It was also to be subjected to criticism, because it was claimed to be unjust and irrational.

Supervision of morals is not possible without knowledge of what is going on in the world. And therefore the theologians – for instance those of the School of Salamanca in the 16th century, when Europe was undergoing a secular inflation just as in the past 50 years – proceeded to engage in the study of causal relations. In a Portuguese manual for confessors and penitents one could read about exchange rates, regarding which it had been discovered that they were also prices and therefore ought to be just. Exchange rates ensure that money is worth the same at home and abroad. According to the manual's author, Spanish gold and silver imports forced prices up. This made him a pioneer of the theory of purchasing-power parity and of the quantity theory of money.

In one of the many works on justice and right, details may be found of the relation between prices on the Flemish and Spanish exchanges. The Flemish Jesuit Lessius, who was a connoisseur of the Antwerp exchange, analysed the effect of supply and demand on the market and listed the causes that, in the opinion of today's economists too, lead to interest being paid on a loan.

The commercial revolution was thus concluded with (often limited) freedom of interest. Henceforth interest was regarded as a price for making money available which was determined by the market or by the authorities. Not only commerce but even banking had become a respectable occupation. What the *communis aestimatio* expressed, it was felt, was natural and just. That also applied to income determination, by which everyone got his due. The fact was that the goods that were managed for God were intended for everyone but, as Thomas Aquinas had written: 'The more prominent a person's position in the community, the more he receives of the common goods for that reason'.

These views of the moral theologians on economic activities served a practical purpose, namely to bring about virtuous behaviour on the part of all the faithful and jointly to realize the ideal of what was viewed as a natural order of society. However, thoughts have also been devoted of old to the promotion of economic activity, with frequent invocation of the public interest, though not infrequently in the service of a particular interest. Right up to the present day such recommendations of a 'sound policy' are usually motivated by a simple philosophy, which even in dark times creates cheerful initiative.

Around 355 BC a report entitled *Ways and Means to Increase the Revenues of Athens* was published. To avoid a threatening deficit on the balance of payments and a deficit of the State, an incentive policy was recommended in the report. The State should invest more in the silver mines and the commercial infrastructure, attract more foreign craftsmen and improve the business climate by giving shipowners and merchants a better image. The Socratic ideal of the good old days was foreign to the author. Trade and industry had to flourish.[1]

Such treatises on how to increase the power and wealth of nations living largely on trade, robbery and extortion were published in large numbers in 17th-century Europe, above all in the developing England.

Merchants and public officials published pamphlets in that country urging that the Dutch be equalled in international trade and driven back. That had to be done by persuading the authorities, who as of old levied taxes and tolls, borrowed money and regulated commerce and crafts, to take measures to protect and promote national industry, commerce and shipping. The natural order of these *mercantilist* writers, as they were called, was perhaps best described by the late mercantilist and contemporary of Adam Smith, Sir James Steuart. Steuart called the modern nations of his day watches that constantly ran inaccurately and therefore had to be repeatedly adjusted by the State (Steuart, 1767).

Even more so than supervision of morals, this political propaganda led to research, or at least to the construction of theories justifying the desired policy. As a result, together with the theologians, businessmen and officials became the first theorists on the operation of the economic mechanism, for even if the watch did not keep good time, one was convinced of a certain systematic relation. Policy is therefore justified not only by its objectives, but also by predictions about the consequences of the measures to be taken. Predictions are justified by explanations. Explanations describe behavioural structures. These were provided for to an increasing extent, though not always entirely altruistically.

By application of the estimating methods of *political arithmetic* introduced by Sir William Petty (1667), quantitative expression was also given to what were regarded as relevant quantities in economic life, such as the total quantity of money in the country, the income per head of the population and the relation between the size of the harvest and its price (price elasticity).

IDEOLOGY

In the second half of the 18th century the descriptions of the system, through the agency of a number of intellectuals, reached the level at which, after concerned wonder, admiration could indeed be earned on a large scale. Newton's completion of the mechanized world view also made itself felt in political economy. In the opinion of the philosopher Helvétius (1758), self-interest assumes in moral philosophy, that is, the philosophy of man and society, the same place as motion in physics. The forces active in the world create equilibrium. In the enlightened view, too, the economic mechanism always runs well – if only the State does not intervene in it. If it occasionally goes wrong somewhere, attempts to step in have a contrary effect. The disequilibria are eliminated by the operation of the mechanism itself. The system is self-correcting: '*Laissez-faire, laissez-passer, le monde va de lui-même*'.

This slogan was proclaimed in France around 1760 by the court physician François Quesnay, although he allowed for exceptions to the rule. According to Quesnay, agriculture was the source of all wealth. The landowners who received its net product in the form of land rent and then spent it were useful distributors of this net product, exclusively suitable as taxpayers. Merchants and craftsmen were useful movers and processors of the products of nature. What the farmers pay to the gentlemen, merchants and craftsmen return to them via what the gentlemen, merchants and craftsmen pay to the farmers. The economic process is one of circular flow, which leads to prosperity if every class, unhampered by the State, performs its task in full and thus keeps the circular flow going. *Physiocracy*, as the theory of the system is called, became a sectarian doctrine of salvation that flourished as part of the French court culture and came to a speedy end. However, the general idea of economic circulation was granted a longer life. Today it is one of the fundamentals of macroeconomics.

The greatest stir was caused by the moral philosopher Adam Smith. Although teaching at a university (Glasgow) with which James Watt was also associated, he was not aware that an industrial revolution had started. His form of industrial production was still the old manufacturing system.[2] In his *Wealth of Nations*, published in 1776, he did, however, proclaim to a series of successive generations the liberal ideology that guided the first phase of the industrial revolution, based on the 'obvious and simple system of natural liberty' (Smith [1776] 1976b, p. 687). True, he wished to emulate Newton, but made so bold as to equate the *desirable* social order with the *existing* immovable order of nature. Nature was a norm.

His rejection of political arithmetic was not very Newtonian either. His line of reasoning was not always consistent, but certainly encyclopaedic, and he supported it with the description of many historical facts. His rational system was nevertheless an ideal that met with a great response from a self-aware and enterprising citizenry. Its influence on politics in the 19th century was very considerable and furthered *laissez-faire* in many, but not all, fields. A school of *classical* economists built further on it.

More Newtonian was the content of his story. It describes, albeit very broadly, the mechanism of interrelated markets, which, through the competition of supply and demand, brings about an optimum *allocation*, by deciding (in accordance with the *communis aestimatio*) *what* has to be produced, *how* and *for whom*. By division of labour and formation of capital (accumulation), the productivity per man and the total production are increased and prosperity grows. What is saved is invested. For the sake of growth thrift is therefore a virtue.

Smith called the mechanism that he described the 'natural system of perfect liberty and justice' (Smith [1776] 1976b, p. 606). There is no place in it for *pretia legitima*. On condition of free competition the highest possible profits may be pursued in a carefree manner. The operation of the market, not the supervision by the priests, ensures that abnormal profits disappear and natural prices that express the *communis aestimatio* are formed. Smith did not expressly call the prices just, but he applied the term to the system. What is brought about within it is owed to the *communis aestimatio*.

Some 40 years later David Ricardo (1817) transformed the cheerful view of an enlightened moral philosopher into the strict doctrine of a man thinking analytically and in abstract terms, who had been trained in the practice of the stock market. He made generous use of *idealization*. By closing his mind to attendant circumstances and disturbing causes he deduced the workings of the forces that he believed prevailed in the system. He presented his points of departure and conclusions as irrefutable laws.

For instance, Ricardo postulated the law of diminishing returns: by using more land, agricultural production increases to an ever smaller extent as a result of the niggardliness of nature. Neglecting the possibility of technical progress, he proceeded from declining productivity in agriculture because he thought, the best land is the first to be put to use, followed by increasingly poor land.

Ricardo also accepted the population law of Thomas Robert Malthus (1798): that the natural growth of the population is stronger than that of food production. The actual population growth is as a result equal to that of agricultural production and wages do not exceed the (historically changeable) subsistence level. Ricardo deduced from the two 'laws' that in the long run, with continued growth land rent rises, business profit falls and wages remain the same. He had no pleasant prospects to offer the poor, the more so since in his view mechanization, of which he was a conscious observer, necessarily resulted in unemployment. His natural order is dominated by irrefutable laws. Ricardo's sombre conclusions seemed to be confirmed by the misery that the industrial capitalism of the 19th century engendered. No wonder that Thomas Carlyle found political economy a dismal science.

However disputed, Ricardo became an example to later economists through his method. The historical and frequently factual approach of Adam Smith gave way largely to a painstaking and often far-reaching logical elaboration of theoretical models. In these, generous use is inevitably made of idealization, but usually with the admission of more relations, that is, more 'active forces', than in Ricardo. For instance, allowance is usually made for technical progress.

Economic theoretical models may very well be described as axiomatic systems. From a number of premises, theorems are deduced. Disregarding the inventivity that is directed towards finding those points of departure, many economists believed that they were engaged in practicing a deductive science, in which the world is discovered by pure reasoning.

However, political economy did not develop simply by abstract thinking from unquestionable premises to certain conclusions. The one ideology conjures up the other in a world in which interests collide. The contrast between the liberal natural order and the actual misery brought Karl Marx (1867) to his criticism of political economy. According to him, poverty, as demonstrated (as he believed) by Ricardo, is necessarily maintained by the existing system, in which the wage-earners are exploited and the driving force that keeps the system in motion is based on making profit and accumulating capital instead of meeting the real needs of society. Capitalism will be destroyed by its own internal contrasts, and the power of the bourgeoisie will be taken over by the working class, who will introduce socialism and then communism (which are based on collective ownership of the means of production and planned production).

According to Marx – as he had learnt from Hegel – the world is not a state, but a process, in which he believed he could detect a pattern. He thought that he had discovered the laws governing the development of society, which is moved by technical progress and the class struggle. Economic relations depend on relative power. Economic growth manifests itself in capitalist society in an increasing accumulation of capital on the one hand and increasing poverty (*Verelendung*) on the other. The accumulation process is disturbed time and again by the regular occurrence of depressions, which necessarily proceed from the nature of the system and intensify the impoverishment.

In Marx competition does not bring harmony but is a destructive struggle that leads to an increase in scale and the formation of monopolies. It is not the justice of a *communis aestimatio*, as with the schoolmen and the classical economists, that dominates his natural order, but the injustice of a struggle for power that in dialectic manner is a necessary step on the path to the realm of freedom and justice.

EFFICIENCY

Around 1850 the wage-increase trend began in England, a process that still continues today in the industrial countries. Relative power, and with it the operation of the economic system, changed. Marx's *Verelendung* did not occur. Ricardo had warned against attempts to interfere with the system, because after all there is nothing that can be done about conformity to a natural law. The philosopher and social scientist John Stuart Mill (1848), however, proclaimed that income distribution is in fact susceptible to structural changes (Mill [1848] 1965, pp. 199–200). He advocated reforms, such as restriction of the law of succession, tax on increases in unearned rents, extension of education and the admission of trade unions, which until then had been forbidden by law to maintain natural liberty.

The critique of political economy, the comparison between theoretical ideal and practical reality, that had been initiated so radically by Marx, continued to occupy a permanent position in a less revolutionary manner. For to an increasing extent the economists came to concern themselves with what the Austrian economist Eugen von Böhm Bawerk (1884) called the pathology of the system. An outstanding example of this was *trade-cycle research*, which endeavoured to find the causes of economic fluctuations and the means of combating them. Through the development of *welfare theory* it was endeavoured to gain insight into the way in which the working of the ideal market mechanism brings about a social optimum that government policy can take into account.

Political economy became an activity of specialists who were university professors. After the 'marginal revolution' of the 1870s, which led to the development of *neoclassical* theory, they devoted considerable attention to a closer analysis of the decision-making that results in the *communis aestimatio*. In doing so they proceeded from *methodological individualism* and from what Karl Popper called *situational logic*; that is, the combined postulate that social events must be explained by the rational behaviour of the participating individuals, subject to the restrictions of the situation.

For centuries it has been established that the level of prices – and thus the value of goods and services – depended on utility and scarcity.[3] The connection between the two found a further specification in marginal utility theory in Gossen's (1854) first law: the satisfaction obtained from each additional amount consumed of the same good diminishes until satiety is reached (diminishing marginal utility). The marginal utility of a good is the subjectively felt urgency of the need to extend one's ownership of that good by one unit. The marginal utility determines the highest bid price with which someone appears on the demand side of the market.

Rational behaviour is based on the supposition of Gossen's second law: everyone portions out his income in such a way that the last monetary unit that he spends on a certain good yields just as large a marginal utility as the last monetary units that he has spent on every other good (equalization of marginal utility). Everyone spends his income in such a way that it yields the largest possible total utility.

If the utility of one good is higher than that of another, the one good is preferred to the other. We can therefore also explain the principles of marginal utility in terms of 'preferences'. Everyone spends his income on that combination of goods that he prefers to all other combinations that can be purchased for the same amount. The preference schemes that individuals have determine the highest bid with which they appear on the market.

The rationality of economic action thus has a very limited significance. Rational behaviour is maximization of utility under boundary conditions. It is based on the one hand on the assumption of the occurrence of gradual satiety upon expansion of ownership. On the other hand it rests on the principles of a logic of choice. A choice is made in accordance with logical rules, the principal one being that of transitivity: anyone who prefers a to b and b to c prefers a to c. The individuals have organized their preferences in that transitive way. They logically choose at all times the most preferred of what is possible with the available means. Not only the behaviour of the consumers, but also that of the producers (workers, rentiers, entrepreneurs) is interpreted as optimizing. They pursue a maximum income under boundary conditions.

From the postulate of diminishing marginal utility and the generalized principle of diminishing returns, the well-known phenomenon was

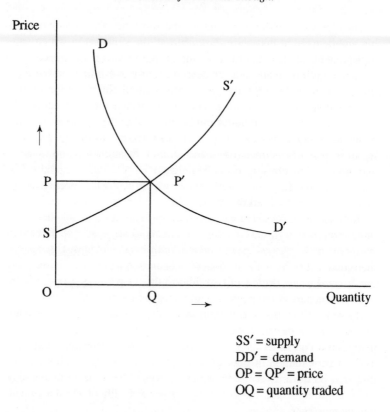

Price

SS′ = supply
DD′ = demand
OP = QP′ = price
OQ = quantity traded

Figure 1.1   The Marshallian cross

derived that at a higher price the demand decreases and the supply
increases[4] The materialization of the *communis aestimatio* on the market for a certain good could be represented by intersecting supply and
demand curves, the *Marshallian cross* (see Figure 1.1). The lower the
price of a good, the more of it will be demanded; the higher the price,
the greater the supply. The higher the sales price of a good, the higher
the prices the producers are prepared to pay for their means of production (including raw materials), and the more will be supplied of them.
The supply curve rises as a result of increasing unit costs upon increasing production. The demand curve falls as a result of the increasing
saturation and the unequal distribution of the wants according to their
urgency and of the income available for this.

The *communis aestimatio* is an equilibrium price that equalizes supply and demand at that price. *Equilibrium*, the situation in which supply and demand are equal to each other, is a central concept in economics, and equilibrium analysis the central activity of economists. With all this an excellent opportunity was created for utilizing mathematics, in particular differential calculus. The optimum behaviour of economic agents in pursuit of maximum utility or maximum profit is nowadays explained in *microeconomics* with an extensive use of maths. This has led to increasingly sophisticated and accurate formulation and to more and more applications in specialist fields.

This rationalization of the *communis aestimatio* has been accompanied by an explicit elimination of justice. The theoretical model led to the conclusion of *consumer sovereignty*. The demand for means of production has been derived from the demand for products. The buyers' demand decides on the destination of the scarce means. Ultimately, therefore, everything in the market depends on the last buyers: the consumers. They decide on the allocation. Departures from this in reality form part of the pathology of the system.

However, the unequal distribution of power of decision among consumers with differing incomes is not a disease, but a symptom of health. The votes that the consumers cast on the market are weighted. They depend on the means available to each, including those from property. As incomes are dependent on prices for services of labour and capital, the votes are, moreover, interdependent. Prices are dependent on incomes, which in turn are dependent on prices.

Interdependence is a characteristic of economic events: costs depend on prices and prices on costs. The market mechanism operates as a signalling system through the movement of market prices and production costs. If costs rise, and as a result profits fall, production of the goods in question is curbed. If prices rise, production is encouraged in certain directions. The market mechanism also operates as a rationing system. Production is limited by the scissors movement of costs and prices and distributed in accordance with the demand exercised.

Léon Walras (1874) designed a theoretical model with which he tried to demonstrate that in a system of interdependent economic units of consumers and producers, the decision-making system of the market leads to what he thought to be a unique result. Equilibrium comes about on all markets. Sellers do not get left with undesired stocks and buyers do not go short of what they are prepared to buy at the current market prices. Identical goods have the same prices. Prices are equal to costs.

Given the available means, technology and distribution of ownership, a maximum of utility is produced.

This analysis of equilibria in economics has the particular aim of explaining changes. In *comparative statics* the changes are described that are the result of the transition from one state of equilibrium to the other. If in a state of general equilibrium the price level is p and the quantity of money m, and if the quantity of money then increases by Δm, according to the model a new equilibrium will be established with a higher price level: $p + \Delta P$. This then explains that prices rise as the result of an expansion of the quantity of money. Not the extent but the direction of changes is predicted by comparative statics.

Joseph Schumpeter (1908) argued that a static equilibrium is in fact never reached. Forces that cause deviations are always active in society. A central role is played in that by the creative entrepreneur who attends to innovation. In Schumpeter's dynamic theory the inevitable occurrence of economic fluctuations is explained by the actions of the innovative entrepreneur. The depression is the price of progress.

Schumpeter devoted great attention to the structural changes in the economic system. His work is an excellent illustration of how in economics the elements of historico-cultural consideration are present. They are well-nigh absent from many economic writings, but in institutionalist works, such as those of John Kenneth Galbraith (1952), they are amply represented. *Institutionalism* is a sociologically oriented form of economic practice that is adhered to by a small minority of economists.

Although an economist and sociologist, Vilfredo Pareto (1906) cannot be numbered among that small minority. He advocated separate practice of the two disciplines, to make them serviceable for application of the method of diminishing abstraction to concrete reality. He removed the cardinal, non-measurable utility from Walras's theory and replaced it by ordinal preferences that are, in principle, measurable. The *communis aestimatio* leads for him to an optimum situation based on the preferences of the participants. In such a state of general equilibrium of the ideal market system, the position of not a single individual can be improved without at least one other individual being worse off (Pareto-efficiency). A monopoly is good for the monopolist but not for his customers. The general equilibrium according to Walras is disturbed.

State intervention in an interdependent market system by levying taxes and spending money (which is decided on by another decision-making mechanism, for instance that of parliamentary democracy) thus reduces the efficiency of the market system.[5] Walras therefore argued that an efficient system need not necessarily be a just one. However, he was of the opinion that a system can be made both efficient and just, namely by government measures aimed at the realization of an ideal market system and by legislation to promote a more equal distribution and partial collectivization of property. Obligatory provision of information by suppliers to consumers on the composition of their products or expropriation of monopolies are examples of improvement of the market system. They increase consumer sovereignty. The foundation of production co-operatives makes the distribution of property more equal and increases justice.

Applied economics ought, in Walras's opinion, to investigate in particular the desirability and possibility of increasing efficiency. According to him, research into the realization of more justice was in addition the subject of 'social economics'. However, in the latter justice had acquired a new content. Medieval man and Adam Smith identified the concept of it with the efficiency of an ideal market system. The natural order of society was, for them, just. Through the agency of the critics of political economy and the social movements since the second half of the 19th century, however, 'justice' now meant a more equal distribution of income, or at least a more equal distribution of property. The ideal market system was, then, no longer necessarily just.

Only the American economist John Bates Clark (1899) revived the classical/liberal idea of justice, which gives everyone his due on account of the social significance of his position and attainments. Clark proclaimed the marginal productivity theory according to which, on the labour market and the capital market, the demand prices of the enterprises are dependent on the value of the marginal product, namely the increase in production that is the result of bringing in one additional unit of labour or capital. However, for most economists his theory was an extension of the existing marginal theory, according to which natural liberty guarantees efficiency but not necessarily justice.

Nowadays a great deal of research is performed in accordance with Walras's formula into the failure of markets – that is, the non-fulfilment of their ideal function – that justifies government measures to improve them. In that failure *external effects* can also play a part, causing defects in the signalling and rationing system.

The opinion is occasionally stated that economists are heedless of the social drawbacks of production, such as air, water and noise pollution. The opposite is true. In 1912, for instance, Arthur Cecil Pigou drew attention to the advantages and disadvantages of production that are not taken into account in the market's decision-making. High costs mean that the production of an article remains limited, but the costs of environmental decay are not included. Conversely, the beekeeper, for instance, receives no remuneration for the improvement of pollination from which the surrounding farmers profit. However, external advantages and disadvantages can be taken into account by collective agreements (for instance with the beekeeper) and if the State improves the efficiency of the market system by prohibitions, regulations, charges and subsidies.

However, research into the just economic system, which Walras likewise desired, is usually kept at bay because it is not considered *free from value judgements*. Today economists explicitly pursue objective research into reality. They make positive, not normative theory. They wish to make their theories available to those who choose their objectives themselves. The ideal of value-free research, as defended notably by Max Weber (1904) for the social sciences, is research that is not dependent in its results on ethics and politics. Weber believed that social ideals cannot be proved scientifically. Consequently, in the view of the great majority of economists, Walras's social economics lies outside the field of economic science.[6] Even in welfare economics the results can be considered to be objective. They are implications of the ideal of the perfect market system.

But economists are only human too. In addition to being industrious persons who do research, they are, as a rule, well-meaning persons with feelings and ideas on how the world ought to be. That came clearly to light with Alfred Marshall (1890), for instance, who was called both a scientist and a preacher by his pupil John Maynard Keynes, and even more distinctly with Keynes himself, who wanted to save Western civilization by solving its economic problems. Come to that, there is not a single great economist whose social and political ideas have remained unknown.

Weberians ascribe a split personality to objective economists. One half examines the world, the other tries to change it. Scientific work is isolated from the other social activities. Marshall simplified that separation by dividing knowledge into two categories. In his view, science was not a real description of the world, but a way of thought. Economics was for him an instrument that can be used to discover the concrete. According to him, economists make an analytical apparatus. They develop a technique for solving certain kinds of problems. Keynes, too, thought along these lines. For him economics, besides being a way of thought, was an art, namely the art of choosing the models that are relevant for comprehending the contemporary world. Economics supplies no knowledge of the world, but is a means of getting to know it. Economists therefore usually call their theoretical research *analysis*.

For Marshall the world was much too complex, and behaviour in the economic domain too greatly dependent on factors that the economist cannot sufficiently survey, ever to be able to describe it with a closed theory. To analyse the interdependence he therefore availed himself of a different method from that of Walras. He attempted it with a *partial equilibrium analysis*. In the latter relations are examined on the assumption that, apart from a few variables of which the behaviour is studied, all others are constant or possess zero value, that is, on the condition of *ceteris paribus*. The partial results are then obtained thanks to extensive background knowledge. Constantly shifting attention sharpens the analytical apparatus for concrete use.

MODERN ECONOMICS

The influence of economists' ideas on the real course of events in the world has always remained limited. Even the principle of *laissez-faire*,[7] by which they had acquired so many enthusiastic supporters and which was supported by so much social power, was never fully realized in the 19th century. In the second half of the century its influence even gradually weakened. Social legislation, the growing power of trade unions and other economic organizations, protectionist trade policy, State initiatives for the founding of public utilities and financial institutions, and the money policy followed by the central banks were so many infringements of the natural liberty of Adam Smith. In 1926 so many serious economic problems occupied the politicians' attention that Keynes could speak of the end of *laissez-faire*.

Ten years later, during a deep depression, Keynes (1936) came forward with a practical solution for the problems that threatened to disrupt the world, based on a new theory. The latter amounted to an explanation of the fallibility of the *communis aestimatio*. In Keynes's opinion the system was insufficiently self-correcting. He regarded the efficiency of the ideal decision-making system as unattainable in reality because decisions on saving and investing are not taken by the same economic agents, and in particular on account of the inherent uncertainty of the future, which destabilizes the expectations of investors. The mechanism of adjustment, which is based *inter alia* on the mobility of prices and volume of production, also operates imperfectly. If a self-reinforcing general mood of pessimism causes investors to shrink from radical decisions, the State, which in Keynes plays a neutral role in society, should promote activity, so as to maintain employment.

The picture of the economic process as a circular flow, which had been developed in the past by the physiocrats and Marx, again became the focus of economists' attention through Keynes's agency. *Macroeconomic* research came to concentrate on relations such as those between income and expenditure flows, levels of prices, interest and profits, quantity of money, stocks, productive capacity and employment. The development of statistical observation was accompanied by a revival of political arithmetic. Practically all nations today possess a system of national accounts, in which detailed estimates of the economic process are recorded.

The new political arithmetic is called *econometrics*. By statistical analysis probable relations between economic variables are estimated that occur in a given area and a given period of time. With their assistance empirical models are made for temporospatially bounded social spaces, so as to demonstrate a theory for the past and make predictions for the future.

Speculating on the stability of the parameters found and the relevance of the demonstrated probable relations in the past, forecasts are made on a large scale, and on behalf of consultation by businesses, social organizations and government bodies the probable consequences of plans and proposals are worked through.

In theoretical analysis, too, mathematics reigns supreme today. Ricardo's method found its consummation in formalization. An economic theory is a set of equations without numerical parameters, the implications of which are derived in accordance with mathematical rules. The formal proof of the theory is often followed by an econometric analysis for empirical support of the theory. In these attempts at furnishing theoretical and empirical proof the scientific aspirations of contemporary economists manifest themselves. With not infrequently the ideal of the natural sciences in mind, many believe that they are applying the hypothetico-deductive method, which is based on the empirical testing of consistent ideas.

This 'scientization' of economics has been accompanied by strong professionalization. Trained in the use of Marshall's analytical apparatus, today thousands of economists find employment in private enterprise and government service. The universities attend to the professional training and form centres of economic research. The *Journal of Economic Literature*, which discusses chiefly English-language publications, lists every year the titles of over 2000 new books, and the *Index of Economic Articles* registers annually more than 20000 articles in a wide variety of fields: general economic theory, history of economic thought, economic history, economic systems, economic growth, economic fluctuations, econometrics, monetary theory, fiscal theory, international economics, administration, industrial organization, agriculture, manpower, welfare programmes and so on. Once the *Wealth of Nations* was a part of the reading of every cultured person. Today economic theoretical writings are accessible only to insiders, who communicate with one another in their own jargon.

There has always been a close connection between the existing economic order and economic theory. Economics is primarily theory of environment: not infrequently it even has a nationalistic slant. Keynes was thinking about Great Britain when he spoke of an economy, and American economists usually mean by an economy that of the United States. Economic science is not practiced in the same way throughout the world. In the countries of the former Soviet bloc, for instance, with their different economic system, other views and problems existed. However, on both sides views on the economy of the outside world were also developed. The study of economic systems and that of the socialist economy in particular is a specialism of the West.

Much greater yet than the size of the theoretical literature is that of applied economic science. The application of economics has expanded more greatly in our days than ever before. Enterprises, organizations and the State collect detailed information on economic life and on the possible solutions of the problems occurring in it. Special research institutes and institutions for giving economic advice to managers of enterprises and the government have been set up for this. The economic technology that they use which, unlike the situation in the natural sciences, is developed almost free of expense and without loss of time, is based on general theories, but often in highly simplified form. Not infrequently general theory is inadequate and the researchers come forward with specific solutions of their own making. The principal activity of an economist consists of writing. The result is a mountain –

impassable by individuals – of memoranda, reports, papers, articles, monographs and books in which the world is described. Economists write history.

The highly varied theoretical and empirical research displays many common traits that have been formed in the course of history. However, the extremely concise sketch that I have given of it would create the wrong impression if it were to be depicted as a science in which the same degree of consensus is reached as in physical research. On the contrary, economics is distinguished by a rather considerable degree of theoretical pluralism. Different schools of thought have emerged. The development of economics may be characterized as the history of movements, of which I have mentioned only the main ones. Of old, schools and trends have existed among economists that adhere to contradictory ideas.

It would also be incorrect to conclude that today all economics is practiced in a mathematical manner. That is chiefly the case in theoretical economics and numerous applications of it. There are, however, also forms of research that are more historically oriented. The study of business and market development, technical progress and institutional changes, that is to say all evolutionary problems, is of a more concrete nature, which receives more attention through verbal description than measurement. But then, too, analysis and comparison with observation are usually pressed into the service of explanations and predictions with scientific aspirations.

NOTES

1. Consequently it is most unlikely that the report is by Socrates' pupil Xenophon, as was previously assumed (Gordon, 1975, pp. 17–18).
2. The old manufacturing system denotes a form of production in which the products are made on factory premises by hand, with the aid of tools and simple pieces of equipment. By the division of labour, productivity was stepped up considerably, as in Smith's example of the pin factory, derived from Diderot's *Encyclopédie*. The size of the business remained limited. The industrial revolution began with the use of steam engines, notably the mechanization of the drives of production machinery, and led in many cases to the rise of very large firms.
3. However, most British classical economists and Marx made an attempt to reduce value in some way or another to physical consumption, that is to say, because means of production are produced with labour, to labour only (labour theory of value). It is possible to demonstrate that prices (value) tend towards equality with costs, in this case the value of the means used (labour and means of production). It is therefore possible to assume that the value is *dependent* on the total amount of labour employed, as Ricardo was interpreted.

But value can in no way be expressed in physical quantities, unless the word 'value' is assigned a different meaning, namely that of a physical quantity. 'Value' then means the volume of production in hours worked, as in fact in Marx and Keynes's *General Theory*.

4. However, further analysis reveals that derivation of the negative price elasticity of demand requires an extra assumption, namely that the substitution effect exceeds the income effect of a change in price.

5. The efficiency would not be impaired if decisions on the payment for the services rendered by the State would be made in conformity with the market.

6. The Dutch Nobel laureate Jan Tinbergen does, however, practice Walras's social economics. See for, instance, his: *Income Distribution* (1975).

7. Most economists allowed for exceptions to the rule.

2.   Economics as a Science

ECONOMICS AND PHYSICS

Among economists there is an old belief which, in an extreme form, convinces some that they know the truth. Others are prepared to settle for less, but even in the opposite extreme the idea dawns in their hesitant minds that they are on a special tack. And that is so. For this belief, of which nobody need be ashamed, is that in the 'scientific nature' of economics.

What this is exactly, is difficult to say. I shall therefore not try to do so. For my purpose it makes little difference whether economics, which is usually regarded as one of the sciences, is rightly or not called a science. However, should there be something special going on that distinguishes it from other sciences – and that is so – to avoid any misunderstanding we must bear this in mind when discussing its 'scientific nature'.

Economists have always liked to reflect on physics and often thought that they could see a close resemblance between the two fields. After all, according to Adam Smith and his contemporaries, society formed part of nature. David Hume, who laid the basis for the balance-of-payments theory, believed in accordance with the ideas of the Scottish Enlightenment that man and society must be examined in the same way as nature, and on that occasion declared introspection to be a form of observation. He was aware that there was a difference, but he quickly side-stepped that (Hume [1739–40] 1975, pp. i–xiii). David Ricardo equated his economic laws to that of gravity (Ricardo [1817] 1970, p. 108) and considered his proposition concerning mechanization as a source of unemployment to be just as sacrosanct as the truth of geometry (Ricardo [1821] 1973b, p. 390).

In many an introduction to economics one can read that economists are at a disadvantage to scientists because they cannot experiment, but that introspection and mental experiments make up for a lot. However, they do not explain how non-experimental sciences such as astronomy and astrophysics have nevertheless been able to make such advances. They also miss the point that use is also made of mental experiments in the natural sciences, but – as is inevitable – more for preparation than replacement of controlled experiments.

The neoclassical economist Lionel Robbins, who had great influence on the methodological views of his colleagues, arrived in his comparison at a decidedly favourable judgement on the position of economics. Physicists have the disadvantage, he wrote, that they have to base themselves on premises that have become known only by derivation. Economists, on the other hand, are sure of themselves on account of their simple premises known to everyone. If the conditions of the theory are satisfied, the events that it predicts will necessarily take place. This inevitability of the analysis accords it a considerable prognostic significance, according to Robbins ([1932] 1946, pp. 104–135). Seldom has a simple view of a matter found so much support as the apriorism that he professed, which John Stuart Mill (1843) developed for the first time under the name 'concrete deduction' as a variant of the hypothetico-deductive model of physics.

In our days Milton Friedman has defended a point of view (Friedman, 1953, pp. 3–47) that has been called 'instrumentalist'. As Friedman himself is a leading economic researcher, we may regard it as a representation of the method that he himself uses in his own judgement. Friedman's methodology is an attempt to describe what modern economists do.

According to Friedman, hypotheses or theories are made to perform predictions. A theory is therefore justified by the success of its predictions. The realism – as Friedman puts it – of the assumptions is irrelevant. The serviceability of hypotheses does not depend on their agreement with reality, but on the extent to which the predictions derived from them work out.[1] In his opinion it is precisely good hypotheses that are not realistic.

For instance, criticism has been made of the assumption of perfect competition in the derivation of propositions concerning the behaviour of consumers and business firms. The freedom to gain access to the market as a seller is often limited; there are sometimes agreements between sellers; the information at the disposal of buyers and sellers is inadequate; monopolies occur; buyers are influenced by advertising, and so on. In practice the condition of the perfect market mechanism is seldom or never complied with. However, according to Friedman, the criticism is irrelevant. What matters is testing the propositions derived from the perfect market assumption by comparing predictions with experiences. If, for instance, an increase in a sales tax results in a decrease in consumer spending, the theory works out.

Friedman has himself devised a macroeconomic theory based on the assumption that economic agents make their arrangements by relating them to their 'permanent income', that is, their expected lifetime income (Friedman, 1956, pp. 3–21). With the aid of this he derives a relationship between the quantity of money in a country and national income that makes predictions possible. The question of what we can or cannot observe of the method of making dispositions assumed by Friedman does not interest him. What is decisive is whether the predictions based on the derived connection between quantity of money and national income work out or not.

This positivism with an 'F-twist', as Paul Samuelson has called Friedman's ideas about assumptions, is defended by Friedman in the conviction that in this way he is proclaiming the unity of science, at least the fundamental equality of economics and physics. But in fact the F-twist is an indication of the difference that exists between the two disciplines, as also are the apriorism of Mill and Robbins and Hume's invocation of introspection. It looks very much as if Friedman divides the hypotheses of which a theory consists into heuristic assumptions that are not tested and empirical hypotheses formed with their aid. The empirical hypotheses, such as those on the relation between quantity of money and national income, are used for making predictions and are maintained if the latter work out to a satisfactory extent: that is, they are tested.

TESTING

Formerly economists explained their theories in verbal reasoning, in which they made an attempt to convince the reader of a certain view of the relations between economic events. They were sometimes very eloquent, such as Adam Smith or John Maynard Keynes. In their plea they appealed to shared experience and thus leant force to their arguments. Sometimes they adduced statistical data that confirmed their theories. These figures then represented in the final instance, recorded events, such as coffee prices in Amsterdam, cement production in France or the number of registered unemployed in the Ruhr District. The figures have usually been processed to reflect relations, such as the average price of coffee per month, the index of cement production or unemployment as a percentage of the working population. Sometimes, too, the economists illustrated their story with imaginary figures that served as sample calculations, as David Ricardo did to explain the law of diminishing returns.

Economists speak a lot about quantities, such as amounts and prices of goods and services, sums of money and financial assets, utility quantities or preference rankings. In this century they have, as a result, increasingly switched to expressing themselves in mathematical terms. They had made a start with this by making considerable use of geometric diagrams in their arguments. However, even complete algebraic formalization did not bring about a fundamental change in theory. Mathematics is a language that renders useful services, above all in the analysis of simultaneous relations. It is in many cases more efficient, because it enables more rapid and more accurate conclusions, but it does not give any extra guarantee that what is asserted in theory agrees with the facts.

Anyway, an economic theory purely in mathematical equations is impossible. Mathematical analysis is always embedded in a system of verbal definitions and a verbal explanation of the mathematically represented relations. The formula $dI/di < 0$ acquires meaning if it is added that I = investments and i = interest rate. The formula then says that investments decline if interest rises, and vice versa. This proposition is rendered plausible by stating that costs increase – and thus profits fall – if the interest rate goes up, that therefore the prospects for investors become less favourable if the interest rate rises and that therefore the propensity to invest declines. The motives of economic agents and the plausibility of their behaviour are verbally explained in the theory.

A mathematical cum verbal analysis, just like a purely verbal explanation (possibly with quantitative illustrations), is therefore a contribution to a discussion that is subject to criticism and that, through its elegance and sound reasoning, can carry away the readers like an eloquent wholly verbal argument. To be accepted as a theory it will have to yield an acceptable picture of reality. Any reasoning, whether or not entirely in natural language, will have to arouse the realization that this is the way in which the world (probably) fits together and that we (probably) can build on it when taking decisions for the future.

The confidence that is needed to accept a theory and consequently to reject rival theories will therefore indeed be supported by the testing that Milton Friedman demands. Predictions must work out. The greater the accuracy with which that can be investigated and the greater the confidence that can be placed in the results of tests, the less pronounced the influence will be of the feelings that have been aroused in the argument with other means. The rhetoric of a science with which supporters and opponents are recruited in the debate and the work of the scientists acquire a different nature accordingly as the conclusion of the debate is made more strongly dependent on testing. The degree to which theorists are disturbed by the result of experiments and systematic observation decreases accordingly as less confidence can be placed in the results of empirical research.

To be able to trust tests with a large measure of confidence certain conditions must be fulfilled. The principal one is the *stability* of the events in the domain. This is apparent above all from the discovery of universal numerical constants, such as in physics the constant of gravitation, the speed of light or the Planck constant. Where such fixed relations are absent, the dubious nature of tests is greatly increased, for tests are always dubious. However, sometimes they are dubious to such an extent that the nature of the scientific debate changes as a result.

All tests are dubious because, after all, hypotheses cannot be tested separately. For the performance of a test the observations of concrete events must be compared with the theoretical description of them, that is, the prediction. However, a concrete event cannot be described with the aid of one single hypothesis. Hypotheses are abstract. Concrete events are theoretically reconstructed by a synthetic combination of various hypotheses. The hypothesis to be tested must be reinforced by supplementary hypotheses to be able to reproduce reality (approximately).

Anyone desirous of performing an experiment to test the hypothesis of gravity takes into account *inter alia* that particles are moved by three other forces as well. The concrete event is then described as the resultant of a number of forces, which can be calculated with the aid of the physical constants and quantities derived from them. Testing takes place along the lines of partial equilibrium analysis, namely by assuming that the probably relevant supplementary hypotheses are true.

To observe concrete events we must moreover use instruments and techniques. What we then observe are interpretations of what is produced with these aids. They are dependent on hypotheses. Someone who interprets an optical image in a telescope mirror as a star trusts among other things a series of auxiliary hypotheses that explain the working of the observational instrument.

In order to test a hypothesis, we thus assume that all other hypotheses are true. However, if the prediction is then disproved by the observation, it is not logically necessary to assume that precisely that one hypothesis is not satisfied. An anomaly has simply become apparent with regard to a complex of hypotheses. For the researchers a problem has arisen that they must try to solve by changing the complex and performing new experiments or systematic observations. For someone who achieves positive results with the experiment there is reason to see their hypothesis confirmed; someone whose results are negative can hold the complex responsible for this.

In physics this method of testing by trial and error is applied with great success, thanks to the stability of nature which imposes on the researchers a large number of limiting conditions that restrict a successful choice in successive situations. Tests are not detached, non-recurrent events, but form processes in time, in which variable complexes of hypotheses are put to the test via a procedure of guessing, searching and shifting. The possibilities of manoeuvre are limited by the fixed points offered by physical constants. In this way a steadily more accurate pattern is woven, in accordance with which the events in the domain seem more or less to take place. Testing is a historical process: creating and correcting, a net is knotted in which more and more facts are trapped.

Testing consists of the inspection of predictions. However, it is not the predictions that are tested, but the explanations. For simultaneously with the predicted events, the fulfilment of the *initial conditions* thereof (which according to the theory have the predicted events as a 'result') is inspected. Predictions are always conditional. If the correlation of initial conditions and predicted events can in fact be established, the explanation is confirmed. If the correlation is lacking, that is a reason for doubting the explanation. Partial equilibrium research then acquires an additional problem that will have to be solved in the long run.

However, there are pronouncements that cannot be doubted. That it will rain or not rain tomorrow is undeniably true whatever the word 'rain' may mean. The truth of tautologies is final. A theory from which it can be derived only that if at a specific point in space and time interest rises, investments decrease or not, speaks the truth but predicts nothing. The explanation cannot be tested because it yields no predictions.

A tautology has no empirical content. Problems must be solved with means that may yield new problems. A testable explanation is refutable. Acceptance or rejection of a theory can be decided upon only if the theory excludes possible results. 'It will rain tomorrow' is a testable hypothesis (assuming that 'rain' can be operationally defined), because the pronouncement excludes the possibility of its remaining dry. The proposition, true or false, has an empirical content.

Theories are made to solve certain problems. For that purpose hypotheses are introduced with implications that relate to still more configurations of events than were taken into consideration in the formulation of the problem. An explanation concerns more events than those calling for an explanation. Someone who explains the toppling of a tree by a gust of wind implies a larger number of events that a gust of wind brings in its train. Broken window-panes, scudding clouds and a blown-off roof could contribute to the proof of the explanation.

A misunderstanding on the part of many economists, which was initiated by John Stuart Mill, is the opinion that in economics fundamental hypotheses, for instance that of maximization of profit, can also be directly tested. The opposite is true: tests are always inspections of implications. Anyone who believes that he is testing the hypothesis 'directly', is in fact examining an implication of it, for example: 'The answer to the question to an entrepreneur of whether he is pursuing maximum profit is in the affirmative'. Anyone who believes that he has to see in the answer 'no' a refutation of the hypothesis will, mindful of the fact that a hypothesis cannot be tested separately, have to take into account for instance the possibility (auxiliary hypothesis) that entrepreneurs do not know what they are doing or that they are leading pollsters up the garden path.

Theories are tested by inspecting their implications. As a result, a testable theory also brings new facts to light, that is to say it draws attention to events that have not been noticed so far. Through his hypothesis about the mass of light, Einstein heralded the deflection of starlight as it travelled close to the Sun which can be observed in a total eclipse. No one had ever looked at this, but his prediction was confirmed by observations.

Under certain conditions that render human intervention possible, with the aid of theories new facts can also be *created*, namely by applying theories. A transistor radio is a new fact that was discovered by the application of new theories. The phenomenon expected by Einstein must already have occurred before. However, an electric motor did not exist previously. The technology that we have developed is an empirical proof of the awesome growth of testable science which, thanks to the stability in the physical domain, was brought about by partial analysis testing by trial and error. Our daily use of those applications constitutes a large, successful experiment with the theories forming their basis.

Research is in fact a continuous discussion of the consistency of theories: formal consistency insofar as the discussion relates to the logical cohesion of what is asserted in joint theories; material consistency insofar as the agreement of observations with theories is concerned. If the discussion leads to the conclusion that a theory is formally and materially consistent, the research is called *objective*. This, of course, is not the same as 'certain' or 'true', for the continuing research can afterwards lead to rejection or amendment of the theory in question.

Such an objective result is seldom, if ever, fully attained. For general testing of the hypothesis complex is impossible, and science is always on the move. A general equilibrium in which all theories tally with each other and with the facts, does not occur. Objectivity is an ideal that can be more or less realized. Because research is a process in time and is never completed, 'the state of the art' is always based on a snapshot of an incomplete state in which many problems are unsolved, many stopgap (*ad hoc*) solutions are found, speculations are made and mistakes are perpetrated.

A philosophical metatheory of short-term scientific growth will therefore inevitably have to make allowance for numerous encroachments upon the principle of objectivity. In a long-term growth theory, on the other hand, this does not need to be done. The movement is in the direction of objectivity. Research directed towards formal and material consistency is an approach to objectivity.

Milton Friedman is of the opinion that in economics such research is done that, as in physics, tends towards objectivity. In his view theoretical pluralism is in the long run cancelled by continued experimental research. According to him economics is an objective science which renders possible predictions that work out.

LOGICAL STRUCTURE OF ECONOMIC THEORIES

In economics relations are postulated, for instance: 'if income rises, consumer expenditure increases' (1); 'if interest falls, investments increase' (2). It is not stated by how much consumption rises if income increases by a given amount, nor by how much investments increase if the interest rate falls by a certain percentage. Something is, however, said about the direction of the change, which is positive (the two variables in the same direction) in the case of the consumption function (1) and negative (the two variables in the opposite direction) in the case of the susceptibility of investments to the interest rate (2). In (1) the further restriction is added that the increase in consumption will always be less than the increase in income.

The restrictions made seem sufficient to test both proposition (1) and (2). After all, for a series of years we can, with the aid of statistical data concerning consumption, income, interest and investments, compare changes in those quantities with each other and then arrive at a pronouncement on the assumed connection. The propositions seem testable because events are excluded by them. They would be contradicted by the facts if consumption falls or rises more strongly than income in the case of an income increase; if consumption does not fall or falls more strongly in the case of a fall in income; if investments do not fall in the case of a rise in interest; and if investments do not rise in the case of a fall in interest.

But we would then lose sight of the fact that hypotheses cannot be tested separately. There are still more influences that make themselves felt. However, the available supplementary hypotheses about these, with which a satisfactorily accurate picture of the concrete events could be constructed, are insufficient in number in economics. It is therefore said that economics is an *aspect science*: it describes an aspect of the events and when used must be supplemented by other knowledge (that is likewise inadequate). Insofar as supplementary economic hypotheses are, in fact, available, they moreover lack numerical parameters with which resultants could be calculated.

Social events are determined by so extensive a complex of causes and are subject to such rapid historical changes that the theoretical reconstruction always exhibits large gaps. The usual comparison with meteorology only partly holds good here: meteorology has physical constants and is consequently testable. It is less complex; its domain is not subject to unpredictable rapid cultural change.

Nevertheless, economists do have methods at their disposal with which they can describe concrete events by the synthetic combination of hypotheses and with which they can make predictions. In their theories they postulate relations that, though not absolutely constant in time, are fairly 'stable', that is, change little in a given space of time. They thus assume that such a relation is the resultant of a complex of causes in which, however, the fluctuations practically cancel each other out. The resultant variation in the relation is small and 'chance'.

In France the consumption function is influenced by unspecified circumstances, habits and customs different to those in the Netherlands, but both in France and the Netherlands, it is assumed, their changeability is limited. If the necessary statistical time series are available, it is possible, taking into account the influence exerted by a number of other events, to estimate the separate consumption functions for the Netherlands and France. For both countries approximate predictions can be made with these for a changing income.

In economics there is little scope for experiment, principally because of obstacles of an ethical–political nature. In such cases, as in other sciences (medicine, for instance), the estimates must be obtained from systematic observations, that is, by statistical analysis of numerical reports (measurement) of events and situations. In economic research the reporting is in the first instance often done for other than scientific purposes, which may entail definitional problems and inaccuracies and require further processing to reduce the inaccuracy.

Because in economics in general there is an insufficient availability of supplementary hypotheses for a complete explanation, the econometrician tries to describe concrete events by distinguishing systematic from chance causes or 'disturbances'. The latter also include the inaccuracies of observation. The systematic causes are represented by the behaviour of one or more independent (*exogenous*) variables.

To keep to a highly simplified example, we may imagine that the annual total consumption in a country (C) is made dependent on the disposable income, that is, income after tax and deduction of social contributions. Because it may be expected that wage-earners have different consumption habits than the self-employed, who run greater risks and therefore save more, we divide the disposable income into that of wage-earners (L) and that of non-wage-earners (Z). The exogenous variables L and Z then indicate the systematic causes. The *endogenous* variable C is the quantity to be explained.

Now suppose that we have available the annual figures of consumption and disposable income of wage-earners and the self-employed in the Netherlands in the period 1950–1980. We can then look for a *specific model* for the Netherlands in 1950–1980, represented for instance by the linear equation $C = aL + bZ$, in which the coefficients a and b are constants of which the econometrician must find the numerical values by statistical analysis. In accordance with this specific model, the consumption in a year (C) is then explained by the behaviour of L and Z.

The formula tells us that C can be calculated by multiplying the disposable income of wage-earners in the same year by a and that of the self-employed by b and then adding together the two amounts found in this way. This specific model is an *interpretation* of the *basic theory* of the consumption function, according to which consumption depends on income. The basic theory is considered to be of general application. The specific model has a temporospatially limited validity. It relates to the Netherlands in 1950–1980. Every basic theory is matched by a large number of interpretations.

Now suppose that the econometrician has found values for a and b, as in: $C = 0.9L + 0.6Z$. The values of C calculated with the aid of this formula will then display deviations from the actual values of the consumption in each year. However, the econometrician has determined the coefficients in such a way that the deviations may be regarded as 'chance'. If he has, for instance, applied the method of least squares, the deviations upwards and downwards will cancel each other out if the whole period of 30 years is considered.

The estimated equation characterizes a pattern in accordance with which the events examined have taken place in a certain period. However, it does not necessarily mean that a sufficiently accurate pattern has been found. The differences between the calculated and the actual values of C may be so great that only a small part of the actual consumption is explained by L and Z, and the estimated parameters ($a = 0.9$ and $b = 0.6$) may be highly unstable. They would be perfectly stable if we were to split the period of 30 years into separate parts and were then to find every time for each part the same parameters as for the whole. The accuracy and stability of the pattern can be established by the econometrician by calculation of a few indices.

What the econometrician aspires to is the best interpretation, that is to say as accurate and stable a model as possible. He tries to achieve this by trial-and-error research in accordance with the empirical scientific methods of partial analysis. For this purpose he varies the specification of the model. For instance, he can change the choice of the variables. Thus it is conceivable that in our example the variable R (= interest rate), which has a positive effect on saving and hence a negative one on consumption, is added: $C = aL + bZ - cR$, or that it is not the absolute amounts of income and consumption that are compared with each other, but their annual percentage growth. The econometrician can also introduce lags. It is, for instance, conceivable that the consumption in a year is made dependent on the disposable income in the preceding year: $C = aL_{-1} + bZ_{-1} - cR$. He can change the mathematical form, for instance by substituting CR^2 for cR. He can apply many other variations too. The specific model is therefore not a faithful reflection of the basic theory. It is not an *instance*, but an *interpretation* of it, that is, the specification is not strictly prescribed by the basic theory, but is based on a choice by the researcher out of many possibilities that are allowed by the theory.

With such a model predictions can be made. These are based in fact on an extrapolation, namely an application of what has happened in the past to the future. The basic assumption is that the pattern of the events that has been found for a period is a lasting one. The predictive force of a comparison is then assessed *ex ante* on the strength of the reliability indices, but must of course be confirmed by experience. The model with the most stable parameters does not, in fact, always yield the best predictions.

Most econometric models are of such a nature that prediction is not possible on the basis of the knowledge of what has already happened. A physician can often predict the future course of a disease on the basis of observed symptoms. In the variant of our simple model into which lags have been introduced, it would be possible – if the data on income are known quickly enough – to predict the consumption in the current year. However, usually the quantities to be predicted are largely dependent on a synchronous – at least not previously known – fulfilment of the initial conditions. These are then estimated on the basis of available information, surmises and guesses.

The predictions with an econometric model are therefore in fact provided with a specific *ceteris paribus* clause. The 'scientific' prediction is partly based on subjective expectations. The prediction runs, in fact, as follows: *assuming* that a number of specified conditions have been met, the following events will take place. If, for instance, there is a story in the paper that according to predictions exports will rise by X per cent and unemployment will fall by Y per cent, this may mean that *if* exports rise by X per cent – and they probably will – unemployment falls by Y per cent. Economic predictions are therefore partly dependent on subjective guesses. Like those of businessmen, the guesses may be optimistic or pessimistic. The force of an economic prediction lies less in telling foresight into events than in a consistent view of them.

To *test* a model such subjective estimates are not necessary. No predictions for the future need then be made. If the values of the exogenous variables are not known in advance, for the sake of testing a prediction is made after the event based on the actual values of the exogenous variables. The theoretical (predicted) values of the endogenous variables are then compared with the values meanwhile attained. The actual rise in exports is then taken as a starting point for calculation of the theoretical value of the relative change in unemployment in the same year. If the test does not yield satisfactory results for a series of years, the model will have to be revised.

Negative results of a test thus lead to the conclusion that the interpretation of the basic theory must be amended. But the basic theory itself also qualifies for critical consideration. If it should then be decided to change the basic theory, however, in the discussion little evidential value can be derived from the testing. Perhaps the interpretation was wrong, and not the basic theory. The negative results may give rise to rejection, but do not make it obligatory.

A negative result of the testing confronts the economic researcher with a dilemma. If he concludes from the rejection of the specific model that it must be changed, he assumes that the basic theory is true. If he concludes that the basic theory must be changed, he assumes that he has chosen the correct interpretation of an untrue theory. In the discussion, the position of supporters and opponents as they invoke the test results is much weaker than in physics.

Usually the econometrician opts for the first point of view: the basic theory is accepted. In that case he does not test, but estimates. He applies the basic theory to illustrate it or to assess a situation in the light of the theory. For a plausible theory he seeks support in the facts, but does not put it to the test. If he opts for the second point of view, he is deficient as an empiricist in power of conviction.

The cause of the dilemma lies in two deficiencies that are interrelated: economics does not have any universal numerical constants and insufficient supplementary hypotheses are available to reconstruct concrete events and situations theoretically. Without these deficiencies it would be possible, as in physics, to make specific models that are not interpretations of basic hypotheses but instances of them. Then, too, there is a choice upon refutation, but this relates solely to the complex basic theory, which consists of hypotheses, supplementary hypotheses and auxiliary hypotheses. Then, too, there is scope for obstinate belief on the part of scholars who do not wish to put aside certain hypotheses.

However, once one has finished discussing the reliability of the experiment, the difference of opinion is fought out entirely at the level of the basic theory.

According to Imre Lakatos (1978) there is a hierarchy of hypotheses, in which the higher placed ones do not enter into consideration for revision until no further progress is made in any other way. In economics the hard core of highly placed hypotheses can encompass the complete basic theory.

On the strength of the similarities which undoubtedly exist, it may be established that the problem of testing in economics does not differ *fundamentally* from that in physics. In both cases there is no question of testing individual hypotheses, but a complex of hypotheses. The difference is one of *degree*. The complex is considerably expanded in economics by the assumptions of interpretative specific models. The instability in the domain makes a clear choice of theory and model on the basis of tests impossible. Not infrequently specific models are based on rival basic theories without being hardly inferior to one another in predictive force.

The rejection of a specific model creates no problem in basic economic theory. The latter can be maintained with instructions to the researcher to seek a better specific model or perhaps even, as the neo-Austrian school of economists demands, to halt such a search because such a model will not be found after all on account of too many variable factors being involved. As a result of all this, economics is less objective, that is to say necessarily remains much further away from the ideal in its results. The difference between economics and physics is not a fundamental one, but it is very great indeed. A comparison of the logical structure of economic theories with that of physical ones shows that Friedman's physicalistic view of economics does not hold good.

NOTE

1. On the strength of this we must conclude that hypotheses are thus realistic. However, Friedman seems to mean that, of the fundamental hypotheses, only part of the deducible predictions is taken into account in testing. His fundamental hypotheses are *ad hoc*. They are relevant only insofar as predictions can be derived from them for the reconstruction of events to be explained. Should a survey show that entrepreneurs do not pursue maximum profit, that is to him no refutation of the hypothesis of maximization of profit to explain price movements. If prices behave as predicted, the theory is in order.

3. Economics as a Philosophy

FALSIFIABILITY

According to Karl Popper the growth of science is a rational progress occurring in accordance with the rules of a method. Science is an undertaking in which risks are taken. Its growth is not an accumulative inductive process that happens as an endless series of successive verifications of increasingly exact propositions. Universal statements cannot be verified.[1] On the contrary, they are bold assertions that must stand the test of criticism. They are not proved logically, but their rationality is ensured because they can be refuted in accordance with the logical rule of the *modus ponens*. In principle the solution of every problem is therefore provisional. A solution is accepted with risks and maintained as long as it is not falsified and explains more than another solution. A new solution must be sought if the old one is rejected. That presentation of the case seems acceptable to me, but with at least two reservations.

The first is that Popper's view cannot be other than a long-term metatheory. It represents an ideal. Finding new, successful theories depends on talent, chance and time. Decisions to accept or reject theories are, as a rule, not fleeting events, but processes. Sometimes it can take as long as a century before a problem is solved. In the meantime – and we are always in that – we must also make do with breaches of rules, *ad hoc* solutions, steps back and mistakes. The reality of research is much messier than the ideal.

The second is that falsifiability must be regarded as a logical property, viz. as refutability on condition that all supplementary hypotheses and auxiliary hypotheses are true. That does not mean – according to Popper either – that if an anomaly is brought to light the hypothesis in question should logically be rejected. It does mean that the testing of the hypothesis by partial analysis must logically be able to yield a new problem with regard to the complex of hypotheses. Hypotheses that, however the tests work out, never compel revision of the complex are non-falsifiable. They should be able to produce an anomaly, otherwise they have no empirical content and cannot contribute to the information that the complex contains.

According to Popper's ideal of rational growth, the development of science is governed not only by the creativity of scholars, but also by their criticism. Criticism is an attempt at refutation. In empirical science, it consists in immanent criticism (logical analysis) and intersubjective testing. The former is directed towards assessment of the formal consistency; a theory that is logically sound qualifies for acceptance.[2] The latter, the empirical criticism, is directed towards assessment of the material consistency. A theory that for everyone who is sufficiently schooled does not prove to agree with the 'facts' is falsified; a theory that is falsifiable but passes every test and explains more than available alternative theories is accepted.

The testing leads to a description of events and a comparison thereof with the description of the events that ought to take place according to the theory. According to the theory, if the initial condition I is fulfilled, the predicted event P will occur. If the observed events I' and P' agree closely enough with I and P, I' and P' are implied in the theory. The theory is not refuted.

A history of a critical science in which the ideal is realized to a great extent may be described as a process of progress. The theory becomes increasingly better. The agreement with the facts becomes steadily greater through the constant revision of the hypotheses and ever stricter tests, and more and more mistakes are eliminated. Because in the emergence of an anomaly more than one hypothesis can qualify for revision, there is, however, little chance of a straightforward development. According to Imre Lakatos (1978) it is thus not theories complete in themselves that succeed one another, but research programmes in which a limited group of hypotheses is considered for revision as long as the execution of a programme displays progress and a hard core of hypotheses can stay unaffected.

In recent years various attempts have been made to describe the history of economics as a Lakatosian process. The economic schools that have succeeded one another in the mainstream, such as those of the classicists, the neoclassicists and the Keynesians can, with not too much effort, be classified as research programmes. Because of the prevailing conviction that Lakatos is an authoritative philosopher of the natural sciences, the application of his metatheory again reflects a physicalistic interpretation of economics. Economics, it is felt, develops in the same way as physics. However, an objection must be made to this idea of things. The special problems of testing in economics, which relate to interpretative and not to instantial models, also make its development different.

ECOLOGY

Critical science that can develop in accordance with the principles of a method displays autonomous growth. However, science is practiced in an environment. It forms part of culture, which comprises everything that man learns and creates. During the history of mankind, critical science has developed in a temporospatially limited area. Its growth is evidently dependent on circumstance. It can exist only in a society in which it is recognized that existing views are open to improvement. Today the circumstances are almost ideal. Science is no longer simply tolerated but even encouraged, *inter alia* because increase in production, human life span and power is expected from its use. Marx designated science a productive force.

However, even in a tolerant society science is not practiced in complete independence, that is to say driven along solely by immanent and empirical criticism. Theories cannot be derived from the facts, as naive inductivism would have it. They are *postulated* and then critically examined. They are repeatedly revised in order that the facts will fit them better. They are based on ideas that are corrected with new ideas with reference to nature's answers to the theorists' questions. Hypotheses emanate from ideas, analogies and inspirations, but must meet nature's boundary conditions.

The inspirations of the theorist may be influenced by ideas developed in other fields of culture. Conversely, scientific theories can exert influence on ideas in other fields of culture. An example of such fertilized and fertilizing ideas is formed by the *explanatory ideals*, as Stephen Toulmin calls them; namely certain fundamental postulates that form the basis of a series of successive theories (research programmes) and for a very long time are not subjected to criticism (Toulmin, 1972, pp. 150–55). An instance of an explanatory ideal is that of the *mechanism* that governs economic science. The idea of the moral philosopher Adam Smith, who saw a mechanism in society, was formed under the influence of natural philosophers (as physicists were once called) such as Descartes and Newton. Economic models used for simulation and prediction are descriptions of mechanisms. Conversely, an economist has occasionally inspired a natural scientist, as in the case of Charles Darwin, who saw an analogy in Malthus's population law.

The growth of science proceeds in the form of a discussion of problems caused by the solution of former problems. The history of a science is, as Toulmin calls it, a *genealogy of problems* (Toulmin, 1972, pp. 300–307). Discussion is communication. As a result, the development of science is partly determined by the way in which that communication takes place, and depends on numerous social factors, such as education, the existence of intellectual centres at universities and academies of scholars, the organization of research, the possibilities for publication and the surmounting of language barriers.

The organization of science depends in part on the financial resources that society makes available for it. In former times these had to come from philanthropy and moneys paid for study. During his professorship Adam Smith depended on the fees that his students paid him. Today the State largely finances research and, above all where applied research is concerned, a number of industrial concerns also attend to it. Enabled by their financial backers, the scientists form a different group in society, an *Invisible College*, with its own rules of good conduct, admission and exclusion, in which power-forming and power struggle, for instance by appointments, can also take place (Kuhn [1962] 1970).

All these extra-scientific factors from the environment in which science is practiced form part of its *ecology*. Moreover, the scientists have their personal idiosyncracies. Thus the development of economics has been influenced by the fact that François Quesnay was a physician. Karl Marx a Hegelian and Alfred Marshall a timid man.

The many factors can be summarized in a highly simplified schedule according to which culture evokes explanatory ideals, explanatory ideals influence the formation of hypotheses and the formation of hypotheses leads to theories. In turn these theories affect the explanatory ideal and culture. Moreover, they generate predictions that, by daily confrontation with nature, influence the formation of hypotheses. A distinction may therefore be made between two circular flows: a slow one, concerning the relation of theory to culture, and a quick one, concerning the relation of theory to nature.

In Figure 3.1 the bold arrows represent the daily transactions and the light ones the impulses that in the long term help to determine the direction of research. Growth depends on an intensive daily question-

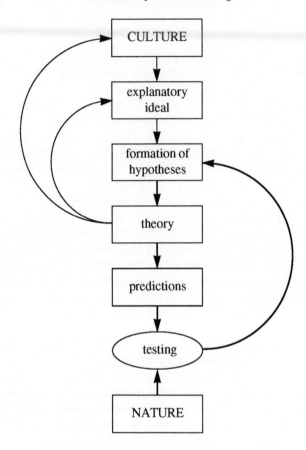

Figure 3.1   Confrontation of culture and nature

and-answer game between researchers and nature, which determines what may be regarded as the autonomous growth of science.

CULTURAL SCIENCE

The schedule, in this form at least, is not applicable to economics. Economic theories do not comply with the requirement of falsifiability. They are of the nature of basic theories, which allow many interpretations. The specific models, like the basic theories themselves, are made in both mathematical and verbal form. In both cases their acceptance or

rejection may normally be decided on in the same way. Whoever decides, on the strength of a certain monetary theory, that in a given year
inflation will rise in the Netherlands as the result of an intensified credit
expansion by the banks, is using a verbal model. If then inflation does
not rise despite the increased creation of money, the prediction has
been disproved and the model falsified, but not the basic theory. The
theorists will plead the *ceteris paribus* clause. The specific verbal model
can be improved.

In a mathematically specific model the predictions have a greater
empirical content. For instance, the model does not predict that prices
will rise more strongly, but that they will rise by more than 4 per cent
over the previous year. This model is likewise falsifiable, but the complex of basic hypotheses forming its basis – purely verbal or not –
contains insufficient restrictions with regard to the admissible interpretations of these hypotheses. The basic theory does not specify which
interpretation is the correct one, but amounts in fact to the pronouncement: 'There is at least one materially consistent interpretation for
every temporospatially limited social space'. This is an existential statement. Existential statements are non-falsifiable; they can be confirmed,
but not refuted.[3]

Basic economic theories do not satisfy Popper's requirement of
falsifiability. It does not logically follow from the failure of a specific
model that the basic theory has also failed, for the specific model is not
an instance of the basic theory. On the strength of his own intuition an
economist can of course decide to reject the basic theory as a result of
repeated failures, but the failure of the specific model was not at variance with the assumptions of the basic theory.

It is true that the proclamation of a new theory is usually accompanied by the statement that the old one is hardly adequate any longer, but
usually this is an outlook inspired by a broad view of the world rather
than the result of painstaking research. Today many reject Keynes's
theory on the strength of experience of its application, without ever
having examined whether in the past it was applied in the right way.
Changes in politics can sometimes be attributed to changes in theory,
but the opposite connection can also be made. Empirical findings usually play a part in the debate on a conversion, but there is never any
question of painstaking testing with a decisive result.

The non-falsifiability is a result of the lack of stability of economic
relations. They are subject to rapid historical change. The structure of
'nature' is largely unpredictable in economics. The number of stable

hypotheses for reconstruction of the concrete events is inadequate. No instantial models can be constructed with them. The 'nature' with which we are concerned in economics is a part of culture. Even if the flow of ideas consists of similar elements, its construction is nevertheless different in economics from its construction in the natural sciences. The feedback from empirical criticism to the formation of hypotheses is much weaker in economics and the influence of cultural change on the formation of hypotheses is much stronger.

The development of economic thought cannot be adequately described without involving cultural and social history – economic history in particular. The performance of economic research programmes is partly dependent on the social hullabaloo. In this connection the

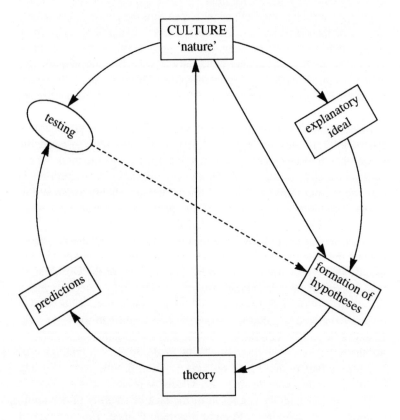

Figure 3.2   Interwovenness of culture and 'nature'

development of pure theory in economics is governed by its application much more than in physics.

Albert Einstein tried to solve a purely theoretical problem by means of his theory of relativity. Conversely, his contemporary John Maynard Keynes concerned himself with a theoretical problem to try to help change the world. Economic theories are to a large extent intellectual answers to variable practical questions. 'In the history of economic thought those count the most who have concerned themselves extensively with the problems that disturbed their generations' (Mitchell, 1967, p. 13). The rational growth process of science and the ecological development are much more interdependent and interwoven than in the natural sciences (see Figure 3.2).

PLAUSIBILITY

The logical property of falsifiability has been proposed by Popper as a demarcation criterion for distinguishing empirical scientific and metaphysical statements. However, with that analytical characteristic no sharp line is drawn between the two fields. It does not take much effort to point to falsifiable statements in a philosophical work and to metaphysical ones in a scientific work. However, the criterion seems usable for denoting a difference of degree.

Every system of propositions contains non-falsifiable M propositions and falsifiable F propositions, but their relative frequency may differ. On the general MF scale, physics is on the F side, philosophy on the M side and economics in between. Because its basic theories are non-falsifiable, economics is of a more philosophical nature than physics, but is also (because its specific models are falsifiable) of a more 'scientific' nature than philosophy. In economics there is more testing than in philosophy and more philosophizing than in physics.

A non-falsifiable proposition is not necessarily untrue. It may therefore be believed with great conviction. Basic economic theories are usually proclaimed with great certainty. Economic theorists do not like using the word 'probably'. The feeling of being in possession of the true insight and being on the right side with one another is not entirely foreign to them. Particularly in the United States the universities are often bastions of economic fellow-believers propagating the truth. Nevertheless, it may not be concluded that, because testing is deficient, rational discussion is out of the question. Nor is testing either an adequate or a necessary condition for a discursive assessment of ideas. In *all* sciences the *acceptability*, that is, the plausibility, of hypotheses and theories is the subject of discussion. Testing is in physics a very strong argument that contributes to the formation of judgements. In economics, through the instability in the domain, it is an unclear and much weaker argument to show the material consistency. However, it does not render a rational discussion of acceptability impossible.

A theory must not only agree with experience. It must contribute to the solution of problems. It must fit into a whole of accepted theories. It must be *coherent* with them. It must offer an attainable solution. As Popper has remarked, a rational discussion can indeed be conducted on such problems of coherence (Popper [1972] 1983, pp. 32–5). There are, after all, problems for which we need solutions, but which can be attended to only in a speculative way.

It is in this light that the apologia for political economy by former authors such as Mill and Robbins must be seen. They posit that economists start from simple points of departure known to everyone by his own observation. Man pursues maximum returns. Marginal utility diminishes as the supply increases. If the supply increases, the price falls. Proceeding from such almost universally recognized facts the economists try to arrive at plausible conclusions on the connection between events. Sometimes, like Ludwig von Mises (1962), they also invoke a rational *a priori*. The principles of the logic of choice are to Mises the principles of economics. According to him economics is an evident doctrine of rational action, a praxeology.

Many see in introspection, too, a source of knowledge. By self-contemplation we recognize the motives explaining human behaviour. Identification with the acting persons is, in the social sciences, in any case a prerequisite for insight into the coherence of their behaviour, as Max Weber has contended (Weber, 1951, p. 428). Empathic understanding (*Verstehen*) is based not only on introspection but also on projecting oneself into a culture.

Even the positivistic attempt by Milton Friedman is accompanied by invocation of heuristic premises. Something is the matter in economics. The realization of the special nature of basic economic theories is evidenced by all these methodological views. Basic theories are in fact *heuristic systems*. They are accepted because they are deemed to give a plausible picture of reality. They are made to generate testable specific models. In explaining them, plausible reasons are adduced.

In this, much use has always been made of the method of decreasing abstraction. First a very highly simplified case is analysed, for instance that of the trade between two countries that both produce the same goods but at different costs. One next assumes more countries and more goods and keeps on introducing more differences. In each phase of the analysis assumptions are introduced that bring the paradigm closer to reality. With the growing realism of the assumptions, the conclusions are then deemed more plausible. Of course, empirical arguments are as a rule not absent but, because they are open to several interpretations in the absence of physical constants, they carry less force of conviction. Only Friedman, who regards the testing as decisive, drops the requirement of realism of the assumptions and considers precisely unrealistic assumptions plausible.

The various views of reality that economists devise are not only based on this kind of plausible argument. They derive their force of conviction from poetry too. Marx sees production as embodied in 'quantities of congealed labour'. Dutch monetary theorists let the creation of money be 'absorbed' by the growth of the national product. Money is something that is 'liquid'. There is an exceptionally large amount of 'flowing' and 'streaming' in economics.

Donald McCloskey (1985) rightly drew attention to the rhetoric of the economists, which is much more than a curious use of language. It is, as in other walks of life, a means of *convincing*. The rhetoric – in the classical sense and not in that of 'false embellishment' – determines human conversation about the things of life. We express ourselves in metaphors to understand each other and the world empathically.

A frequent problem in economics is the extensive use of intensities. We speak of 'quantities of utility' or 'extent of welfare', even though we know that these are not measurable. William Petty compared the value of an Irishman with that of an Englishman, and we do this in almost the same way by calculating the 'income per capita'. We issue a warning to the users that it does not measure what it measures, but theorize away ourselves in unbridled fashion.

We speak of the 'volume' of production, income, imports, exports and consumption, and we mean by it an imaginary value 'at constant prices' but, theorizing all the while, are thinking of quantities of a substance that does not exist. In capital theory a controversy exists about the measuring of capital, which in fact is concerned with the coherence of a metaphor. Economists often think in terms of a mythical jelly. Sometimes they regard it as putty, and sometimes as clay; with these substances they design putty–putty and putty–clay models.

A magic wand of many an economist, with which he transforms the appearance of things, is 'rational behaviour'. This is based on the assumption that an individual does what he chooses to do, and chooses more above less. However, 'choose' is defined as 'what he does' and 'more' as 'what he chooses'. The entrepreneur who pursues growth in this case acts just as rationally as one who pursues maximum profit. The small shopkeeper who leads a poor existence also acts rationally by not accepting a well-paid job. A miser acts just as rationally as a spendthrift. With one tautological touch of his magic wand, the economist can declare the whole world rational.

Very extensive use is likewise made of the market metaphor. Economists are inclined to see social problems in terms of supply and demand. A Schumpeter-inspired modern trend in the economics of the public sector, which explicitly calls itself 'political economy' again, sees politicians acting in an electors' market where they sell promises for votes. When the measurable eludes us, we think in images. It is a way of coming to an understanding and formulating an if possible common view of the world.

VALUE-LADENNESS

According to the ideal of critical science, *objective* theory is pursued. This is accepted purely on the strength of hitherto found (that is, not refuted) formal and material consistency, irrespective of other qualities of the theory such as its aesthetic, moral, political or ideological attractions. A non-objective theory is *subjective*. A subjective theory is not necessarily that of a single individual. It can be adhered to in wide circles. Objectivity is not the result of the researcher's freedom from prejudice, but of a social custom, namely application of the method of immanent and empirical criticism. It is independent of the researcher's properties. It is the result of a certain form of discussion (Popper, 1972, p. 112).

An objective theory describes things, but does not assess them. Assessments are dependent on *values*, based on views of the way in which life must be lived. 'A value represents a slogan capable of providing for the rationalization of action by encapsulating a positive attitude towards a purportedly beneficial state of affairs' (Rescher, 1969, p. 9).

Some values are of an ideological nature and are like banners under which to fight. Values are norms, ideals that must be pursued.

The method of a science rests on a system of norms, and thus on a value too. If it is said that an objective theory is *value-free*, the meaning is that it is free from extra-scientific values. An objective theory of this kind is at the same time a *positive* theory, that is, it describes, not prescribes. It is, however, incorrect to assume that conversely all positive theories are value-free. A biased story is positive, but not objective. It is not value-free, not because it contains *prescriptions* or *value judgements*, but because it meets other than the scientific norms and not these. The frequently voiced proposition that a theory is value-free if it contains no value judgements must therefore be rejected. As R.M. Hare has argued, there is no exclusive difference between what are called 'existential judgements' and 'value judgments'. One can describe evaluatively and evaluate descriptively (Hare, 1952, pp. 111–26).

Objectivity is an ideal that can be attained only if the formal and material consistency of theories can be fully corroborated. However, hypotheses cannot be tested separately. As a result, every science has a subjective slant. It contains a number of ideas that are maintained for a very long time without being put to the test. They give the appearance of what Thomas Kuhn calls a 'paradigm' and Imre Lakatos a 'hard core'. They constitute scholars' views that are accepted for a very long time in a very wide circle. According to Stephen Toulmin, there are thus in physics, too, ideas about a 'natural order'. Newton's law of inertia cannot be corroborated empirically, any more than the assumption that light travels in a straight line (Toulmin [1953] 1960, pp. 57–104).

Every science has its natural order, which is not derived but postulated and for a very long time is not considered for revision. The hard core of ideas relates in the natural sciences to how the world is *seen*. However, the social sciences are concerned with a world that is not only seen, but also *made*. Social science investigates something that we experience and want to change. As a result, the subjective element in the theory is easily bound up with ideas about the way in which life must be lived. In that case the theory is not value-free, but *value-laden*. The view that is set down in the core becomes an ideal: a picture of the world as it should be. In economics that inclination to see in the world not only a state of affairs but also a goal has always come very clearly to the fore. The natural order of the economists was in many cases an attempt to represent not what is in existence but what had to be brought about.

But the realist who wishes to resign himself to how in his opinion the world in fact stands also represents in that way a scientifically unproven view that relates to how life must be lived for want of better. The natural order of society *always* contains an implicit guideline for action. A social science is consequently not value-free.

The most striking ideal of the economists is that of the perfect market mechanism, according to some to be approached as closely as possible by *laissez-faire* and according to others by systematic intervention and correction. Even those who have advocated abolition of the market mechanism return many times, in their attempts to apply their ideal, to measures conforming to market principles and restoration of markets.

According to Léon Walras, all businesses could, if necessary, be nationalized without harm to liberty, equality, order and justice as long as the regulating and co-ordinating markets continued to exist for the sake of efficiency (Walras [1898] 1936, pp. 272–3). The most popular ideal of the natural economic order is that of the market mechanism.

However, within its framework there is still a diversity of views possible that cannot be adequately corroborated by the method of critical science. Rival theories are not decided on in economics by critical testing, but by discussions in terms of plausibility. It is inevitable, in view of the commitment that is evidenced by their concerned attention, that the values that the critical scientists try to keep out are admitted as subjective elements and influence, usually implicitly, the weighing-up of the arguments.

The fact that economics is an aspect science means that the theorist who adheres to certain ideas about the other aspects so arranges his economic aspect that it can form a whole with the others. The way in which man, society and history are regarded penetrates in this way into the economic field of vision. Economics strongly undergoes the influence of social views by the subjective element, which is very great in economics on account of the absence of physical constants and which, by its involvement with man, makes it highly sensitive to values.

All this, of course, does not mean that solely ideological values determine which theories are accepted. Rational discussion relates to too many requirements of coherence for this. Moreover, every science has autonomous 'elements of play' that have developed by tradition and that help to determine the activity of the researchers. Autonomous play finds expression in what Thomas Kuhn calls 'normal' research, which is directed towards consolidation and elaboration of existing theories. Paradigms indicating how the problems must be solved, how the unknown territory must be demarcated and explored, supply the journals with an uninterrupted flow of copy. Sometimes normal economists, through their thirst for adventure in an imaginary world, become alienated even from everyday reality. According to Adam Smith science pursues beauty, fine theory that charms the surprised mind. Today economists may be found who, carried along by the game, are submerged in mathematical beauty.

The value-ladenness of the theory is not explicitly reflected in it. If it is formalized, no value judgement or prescription occurs in the theory. The values in accordance with which we try to organize life we realize as a *sous-entendu* in our creations. Our view of man, society and history can be represented in what we make and without being expressed in so many words. Economics is in part an expression of how we want to live life.

This value-laden subjectivity does not necessarily exclude consensus. Culture can be based on an extensive foundation of unanimity. In an open society like ours, however, differing views usually exist that, through the necessary deficiency of the argument, can be reconciled with one another only to a limited extent. The discussion between the trends even leads not infrequently to mutual reinforcement of the points of view. Sometimes, too, that discussion fails to materialize at all through vast self-assurance on the part of those concerned.

Subjectivity is not an infringement of the scientific method of immanent and empirical criticism. It is, rather, an inevitable component of this method. The same applies to the value-ladenness of economics in particular. This does not do away with the duty of immanent and empirical criticism. Value-ladenness makes of the economist at most a preaching researcher. Even if the possibilities of fulfilment are more limited, the ideal of the empirical scientific method applies to him too. The problems are posed to him by society in terms of cause and effect and with an eye to application. What can be done about inflation and unemployment? How can an optimum investment portfolio be built up with a view to costs, risks and return? What are the consequences of protection for the international distribution of prosperity?

Such problems call for solutions that are empirically supported. The nature of the problems determines the nature of the analysis. The commitment to reality and the risks of application require the greatest possible concrete, specific knowledge. Theories should be formed in such a way that they can be subjected as much as possible to criticism and are most susceptible to empirical interpretation. Economic research is a meaningful but risky business, directed towards knowledge and to the fulfilment of human ideals.

An economic theory is not only for predicting, but also for inspiring with courage. It stimulates risky enterprises. The chances of failure are not inconsiderable, but without the research they would be much greater still. There are, after all, problems that urgently require solutions but that can be tackled only speculatively and with many risks. An economic prediction is a well-thought-out rational gamble that must be considered with daily vigilance and readiness to adapt. So far no better way has been found than that which has been constructed by trial and error over the last 2 500 years.

NOTES

1. The universal statement that all swans are white cannot be verified. If we declare that all swans so far observed are white we do not know whether all swans still to be observed are white.
2. This is the ideal. In fact occasionally, for want of better, theories are accepted that are not entirely logically sound but agree with the observations. It is also possible that, for want of better, theories are accepted that are logically sound but do not fully agree with the facts.
3. The proposition that some Xs are Ys, for instance that some swans are non-white (= at least one swan is non-white), is called an 'existential generalization'; this can be confirmed by tests, but never refuted.

4.   Economics as an Art

NORMATIVITY

The assumptions that are made, notably in the theory of consumer behaviour, concerning rational behaviour are so thin that such behaviour does not reflect rationality in the usual sense. Someone who in the prevailing sense makes a rational choice does more than merely consider whether he is in fact achieving the highest possible ranking in his scheme of preferences. According to Paul W. Taylor, it must be expected of a really rational choice that the latter is made on condition of freedom. The choice is not determined by subconscious motives, and the person making the choice is not subject to inner or outer compulsion. The choice is decisively determined by one's own preferences. It rests on knowledge, power of imagination and practical insight. Scientific and philosophical knowledge is a precondition for a rational choice (Taylor, 1961, pp. 151–88).

In the theory of consumer behaviour economists confine themselves only to the conclusion that man is after what he regards as his preference and to a representation of the formal logic of choice. They do not assert that economic agents carefully weigh matters in accordance with that logic. They merely believe that the behaviour responds to it. The economic principle of rational behaviour is not psychological, as was formerly assumed in a utilitarian spirit, but logical. It relates to *formal* rationality (Gäfken, 1963, p. 26). It also comprises choice under compulsion and on the basis of an incorrect insight.

When one entirely excludes the possibility of irrationality, as Ludwig von Mises does, the proposition of rational behaviour even becomes a tautology. The latter has no empirical content. No predictions can be made with it. It is of importance only to the system of concepts that is used in the economic discussion. Man is then seen as a being who always acts rationally. Anyone who chooses at variance with a choice that he has made before – for instance by now preferring c to a, whereas he first preferred a to b and b to c – does not act inconsistently according to Mises, but has by definition changed his scheme of preferences.

However, most economists assume (often implicitly) that preferences are relatively stable. They do change, but not at any moment. Changes in public taste are changes in schemes of preferences. They may lead to changes in prices. To explain these changes as being from other causes it is necessary to assume that taste is less changeable than prices (Gäfken, 1963, p. 57).

Nevertheless, even if stability of the preferences is assumed, the explanatory effect of the principle of formal rationality is very small. The assumptions that form its basis are so general that their implications with regard to the behaviour of the economic agents are of little importance. To explain the behaviour that is posited in price theory, more hypotheses are needed than that of formal rational choice (Klant, 1984, pp. 126–40).

The behaviour, notably that of the entrepreneurs, is explained by assuming that they make use of rational operational models to solve optimization problems, but the conditions of these models, that is to say their system of values and the information at their disposal, are further specified. It was formerly assumed that they possessed complete information. At present incomplete information and uncertainty about the future are postulated, so that the solution can be found only by using calculus of probability and game theory. Formerly one let entrepreneurs pursue maximum profit. Nowadays other objectives are often (also) taken into account.

Use of operations research in economics is based on the assumption that economic agents usually and by a majority act in accordance with the theory. Rationality is not universal. Irrational action occurs. This assumption that the agents mainly adhere to a system of norms renders applications of the system possible at two other levels.

The first is that of empirical research. The system of norms is then used as a reference point in the description of actual events. What really happens is compared with what ought to have happened if all agents had acted rationally. In this way insights into the degree of irrational action can be acquired, for instance the extent of money illusion (in which the agents do not take into account the effects of price changes on the purchasing power of money). Popper regards this use of situational logic, which he calls the 'method of rational construction' or the 'zero method', as the principal characteristic distinguishing the social from the natural sciences (Popper, 1957, pp. 140–42).

Use of the zero method may be interpreted as a criticism of practice, in other words as a normative application: reality is tested against a system of values. A normative application is even more clearly evident at the second level. For the system of norms is also used and further developed *in the service of the practice* of economic organizations, such as businesses and authorities. It is a different kind of application from the usual one, in which a theory is used to intervene in its domain as, for instance, Keynes's theory for devising an employment policy. That kind of technical application, which has led above all to great successes of the natural sciences, is based on the explanatory and predictive force of theories in terms of cause and effect.

The use in practice of the acting agents themselves is possible only in social science. The system of norms that is used in the theory to explain behaviour is, as it were, extracted from the theory as an independent praxeology so as in this way to justify independent action and deciding oneself on deeds in terms of means and end. The theory of economic action is then used as a system of values for practical action.

Economics as a technological doctrine has been developed particularly in business economics. In the latter, methods are devised and examined for use in the management of organizations, businesses in particular, for instance with regard to their organization, cost accounting, sales policy, financing, use of operations research and data processing.

We are concerned here in part with applied economics, but to a very large extent with the results of separate theoretical and empirical research, as, for instance, is also the case with industrial economics, agricultural economics and the economics of labour. In business economics other disciplines, such as sociology and psychology, are also applied. As a result of all this, business economics is not only a technological doctrine, but also a source from which the formulation of theories in general economic theory can draw for the explanation of behaviour.

REFLEXIVITY

The use of economics as praxeology contributes to the creation of conditions that are postulated in the theory itself. As a result, to a certain extent economics itself summons up the behaviour observed in its domain. The 'spirit of capitalism' or, to safeguard ourselves against the burden of history, the 'economic spirit', is not only observed and explained by economists, but also disseminated by them. The enlacement of culture and nature also makes itself felt in this *reflexivity* of theory and reality. This does not mean to say that economics itself creates the form of conduct that it explains, but that it can *contribute* to the realization of events that it postulates.

According to Gunnar Myrdal, the reflexivity of economic theory is caused not only by praxeological application but also by the interaction of *programme* and *prognosis* (Myrdal, 1958, pp. 159–60). The participants in economic transactions have intentions that are based on, and are adjusted by, their expectations. They have programmes that are made and changed in accordance with predictions that they consider relevant. Conversely, prognoses are made and changed on the basis of what becomes known about plans. It may even occur that, if the public changes its plans on a large scale as a reaction to a prognosis, the prognosis becomes a self-fulfilling prophecy, and also that the prophesized event is prevented by it. The prediction that the United States Bank in New York (with which nothing was wrong) would fail caused a run on the bank in 1928 and, as a result, a collapse. The prediction by an authoritative expert on the stock exchange that prices will rise may cause that rise. A negative effect of a prediction probably occurred in 1947, when a predicted recession in the American economy did not happen, it is assumed, as a result of that prediction.

Even now this does not mean to say that economic prognoses always summon up or nullify the predicted events. Through the interaction of plans and prognoses the theory can exert a certain effect on reality, but only rarely are the predicted events fully summoned up or nullified by it. It is even so that in the theory itself allowance can already be made for the effect of prognoses.

According to Keynes the effect of monetary policy on the interest rate is dubious, partly as a result of the reflexivity that manifests itself in stock exchange transactions. Speculators let themselves be guided more by their expectations concerning the valuations of others than by their own valuation of the securities: market prices come about in part through expectations about the market prices that will come about.

In the theory itself allowance can be made for the effect of prognoses if a systematic connection exists between theory and expectations. In the economic *theory of rational expectations*, which in recent years has acquired considerable support, it is assumed that inflationary effects of expansionary government policy to be expected in accordance with the theory are also expected by the public, the result being that the aim of such an expansion, namely reduction of unemployment, cannot be attained. Economic behaviour is determined by expectations. To the extent that the knowledge of theories influences the expectations, the theory of behaviour can influence the behaviour itself. If that connection is systematic, the effect of the reflexivity can be foreseen by the theory itself.

There is a physicalistic interpretation of economics according to which the reflexivity that makes predictions uncertain is analogous to Heisenberg's uncertainty principle in physics. However, there is no foundation for this superficial platitude. Testing of quantum theory shows that subatomic elements have properties in common in certain situations with particles and in others with waves. As a result of this, a number of formulae are confirmed that Werner Heisenberg derived from the assumptions of the theory, which are called Heisenberg's uncertainty relations.

One of the relations is expressed by the inequality $\Delta p \Delta q > h/4\pi$. In this inequality p and q are usually interpreted as the co-ordinates, the 'momentum' and the 'position', respectively, of a subatomic element. h ($= 6.63 \cdot 10^{-34}$ joules) is a universal numerical constant, namely Planck's constant. p and q are dispersion parameters, viz. of the dispersion of the averages of p and q. The dispersion coefficient is called 'uncertainty'. It follows from the uncertainty relation that if one of the co-ordinates is measured with accuracy (that is, with a low dispersion coefficient), the other co-ordinate can be determined only with great inaccuracy. Nevertheless, the probability of a specific momentum in a given position can be calculated. Quantum theory is not deterministic, but statistical (Nagel, 1968, pp. 293–305).

An interpretation of the uncertainty relation, which has been promoted by a number of pronouncements by Heisenberg himself, but which has been rejected by Niels Bohr and others, is that measurement is influenced by observation. 'Heisenberg's generalized principle', which social scientists sometimes speak of, is based on that interpretation, but in that case no attention is paid to the regular nature of the quantum theory relation. 'Uncertainty' in quantum theory means something different from 'uncertainty' in social science. In no single social science has a comparable relation been found.

'Probability' likewise means something else in the two disciplines. In physics, distribution functions occur with universal constant numerical parameters. In social science they are indeterminate or, if they exist for a specific social space, are relatively stable and non-universal.

Heisenberg's uncertainty principle does not relate to reflexivity. It does not relate to determination of the values of certain quantities, but to their definability. The principle is testable and not falsified after strict testing. It is not a property of the theory, as is the case with reflexivity, but a fundamental constituent thereof.

MORAL SCIENCE

Every science may be regarded as an art, viz. a result of creativity in which expression is given to a form of experience undergone. A theory is not derived from facts. It consists of bold ideas by which facts, which are facts in the light of theories, are trapped.[1] Revolutionary ideas in science are often absurd *a priori*. Newton, Einstein and Planck, like Picasso, teach us to see what we have experienced as new. The surprise that, according to Adam Smith, stimulates research, ends with still greater surprise. The wonders of nature will never cease.

Economics, too, has its highlights that occasion surprise. The banks themselves create the monies entrusted to them. A government deficit can promote prosperity. Pursuit of self-interest in conflict with others may serve those others. Pursuit of entrepreneurial profits causes them to disappear. However, the surprise nevertheless seems to be less in economics than in the natural sciences, for economics solves the paradoxes by explaining events by our familiar human action. We recognize ourselves. The uncomprehended is not explained, as in the natural sciences (and Aristotle notwithstanding), by the incomprehensible, but precisely by the comprehensible. We can identify ourselves with those whom we study. A physicist, on the contrary, cannot project himself into neutrons and photons.

There is not a fundamental, but a considerable difference between economic and physical theories. Physicists find regularities that are described in general theories and specific models that are instances of them. Economists make fundamental heuristic theories embodying views of human action answering to value-laden ideas about a natural order of society. With these theories interpretative specific models are generated that reproduce events in limited social spaces. Economics is therefore in yet another sense more an art than a science, in general. It is a form of historiography. It is based on the art of interpretation. It does not describe laws, but tells plausible tales (McCloskey, 1986, p. 65). It is based on understanding by self-projection.

This philosophy of economics can be brought into line with the views of Marshall and Keynes. As they believed, economics is a moral science, a theory of man and society. It is the art of choosing models that are a supposed relevant representation of contemporary events. The basic theories constitute analytical machinery on behalf of the interpretation of reality. They are less objective than the natural sciences. They mix understanding with desire.

As a result of the absence of supplementary hypotheses or, to put it another way, on account of the complexity of the domain, prediction in economics is also an art. In that case application of the theory is not mechanistic, but is based on choices, notably those of the specific model. Moreover, synchronicity of initial conditions and events to be predicted means that application of the specific model is also based in part on the art of conjecture.

On the strength of the defects of the models and the fallibility of their application, the critics occasionally advocate refraining from prediction. However, given the social need for guidelines and justifications of action, there is insufficient reason for that. After all, in our common endeavour we must make do with speculative, risky and often rival ideas, which we form to give expression to sometimes differing views of the activities in which we participate.

Even the sceptical researcher who is aware of the rapid wastage of theories and the fallibility afflicting, above all, complex theories, need not withdraw his assistance out of disappointment. The development of ancient and medieval ideas into political economy and that of political economy into modern economics has led to a tremendous expansion of knowledge of concrete events. The practitioners of economics are, by a large majority, users of it. Applied economics, above all in this century, amounts to extensive historiography. That is the result of using the theoretical analytical machinery and common sense. As a result we have built up great concrete knowledge, on which policy of organizations, including the authorities, is based.

The empirical research driven along by heuristic ideas has perhaps led to the most lasting results of economic science. If economists were better aware of what they really do, the importance of this could increase still further. Physicalistic pretensions are unjustified and lead to frustrations. An economist is a historian who tells stories about today and tomorrow. He provides us with ideas on goals to be pursued and concrete knowledge about what has happened.

Economics is science, philosophy, art and history. Just as the states-man should possess historical knowledge, so the economist who ad-vises managers of economic units should possess the historical insight that arouses awareness of continuity and constant change. According to Keynes, the economist who wishes to acquire mastery must therefore possess a rare combination of gifts:

> He must reach a high standard in several different directions and must combine talents not often found together. He must be a mathematician, historian, statesman, philosopher – in some degree. He must understand symbols and speak in words. He must contemplate the particular in terms of the general, and touch abstract and concrete in the same flight of thought. He must study the present in the light of the past for the purposes of the future. No part of man's nature or his institutions must lie entirely outside his regard. He must be purposeful and disinterested in a simultaneous mood; as aloof and incorruptible as an artist, yet sometimes as near the earth as a politician (Keynes [1933] 1972, pp. 173–4).

NOTE

1. Facts are facts in the light of other theories (supplementary and auxiliary hypotheses) than the theory (hypothesis) that is being tested. The opinion sometimes proclaimed that theories create their own facts is incorrect.

PART II
Elucidations

5. The Core of Economic Methodology

REFUTABILITY

In empirical science hypotheses are empirically tested. Hypotheses yield predictions which are always conditional. If an initial condition is being fulfilled the predicted event will occur according to the hypothesis: $I \rightarrow (H \rightarrow P)$ or what is the same: $I \& H \rightarrow P$. From the hypothesis, H, and the initial condition I, the prediction P follows. Physicists create an experimental situation in which $I \& H$ are realized and look whether P occurs. However, controlled experiments are not always possible. In that case systematical observations can be made of situations $I \& H$ which occur in reality.

Hypotheses are idealizations. They describe what occurs under ideal conditions. Galileo's law is about the free fall of a body in a vacuum. No disturbing events occur. Additional hypotheses are therefore required to construct the experimental situation. The ideal condition must be fulfilled by approximation. Apart from these supplementary hypotheses, auxiliary hypotheses are employed for observation. An astronomer relies on optical laws when interpreting his observations. Karl Popper calls these supplementary and auxiliary hypotheses the 'background knowledge', and the observed events 'facts in the light of theories'. The occurrence of the predicted event follows from the main hypothesis and background knowledge, B: $I \& H \& B \rightarrow P$. A model which describes real events, which I call a *specific model*, always contains more than the hypothesis or set of hypotheses (theory) on which it is based.

When confronted with an alternative hypothesis the experimenter chooses a prediction from H which contradicts the prediction in the same situation derived from the alternative hypothesis H'. However, such a crucial test is impossible according to the physicist Pierre Duhem. Hypotheses cannot really be refuted, because it is not possible to decide whether the failure of a prediction is due to a faulty main hypothesis,

H, or a fault in the background knowledge, *B*. This was not a reason for
Duhem to stop testing, but an argument for instrumentalism and con-
ventionalism. Theories which are chosen are mere instruments for making predictions. Their choice rests upon conventions. Duhem pleads for
testing and 'good sense'. The disputes between scientists come to their
end because ultimately will be chosen 'a simple, elegant, and solid
system'.

> Pure logic is not the only rule for our judgements: certain opinions which
> do not fall under the hammer of the principle of contradiction are in any
> case perfectly unreasonable. These motives which do not proceed from
> logic and yet direct our choices, these 'reasons which reason does not
> know' and which speak to the ample 'mind of finesse' but not to the
> 'geometric mind', constitute what is appropriately called good sense (Duhem,
> 1976, p. 59).

The logician Willard Van Orman Quine, in his quest for the true nature
of analytic and synthetic, arrived at a more radical conclusion than
Duhem. 'The unit of empirical significance', according to Quine, 'is
the whole of science' (Quine, 1976, p. 59):

> Our statements about the external world face the tribunal of sense experi-
> ence not individually but only as a corporate body (Quine, 1976, p. 58).

Total science, logic included, should be justified by one holistic test
which is impossible.

Quine was a logician and not a physicist. So he does not worry much
about the status of empirical testing by scientists. It seems, however,
that he considers this activity 'pragmatic':

> I espouse a ... thorough pragmatism. Each man is given a scientific herit-
> age plus a continuing barrage of sensory stimulation: and the considera-
> tions which guide him in warping his scientific heritage to fit his continu-
> ing sensory promptings are, where rational, pragmatic (Quine, 1976, p. 63).

Pragmatic in fact is also Popper's point of view. 'Methodological rules
are ... regarded as *conventions*' (Popper, 1959, p. 53). He admits that,
'anything like conclusive proof to settle an empirical question does not
exist' (1988, p. xxii). Nevertheless, scientists decide on empirical tests.
Scientists do test, whatever the philosophers may say. Popper stresses
that a rational progress of science rests on *criticism*, which consists of
four different lines:

First there is the logical comparison of the conclusions among themselves, by which the internal consistency of the system is tested. Secondly, there is the investigation of the logical form of the theory, with the object of determining whether it has the character of an empirical or scientific theory, or whether it is, for example, tautological. Thirdly, there is the comparison with other theories, chiefly with the aim of determining whether the theory would constitute a scientific advance should it survive our various tests. And finally, there is the testing of the theory by way of empirical applications of the conclusions which can be derived from it (Popper, 1959, p. 32).

The second of these lines implies that hypotheses should be refutable by empirical tests. They should be falsifiable, that is, in the light of the foregoing, they should be falsifiable on the assumption that the background knowledge is true.

If a hypothesis is falsified a solution might be found in an amendment or replacement of the main hypothesis, *H*; but also the supplementary hypotheses (even in some cases an auxiliary hypothesis) may qualify for a change. Testing and subsequent adjustment are not a matter of pure logic, but of logic and good sense, ingenuity, intuition and aesthetics.

Not *H* but the complex *H* & *B* is falsifiable. Usually *H* is chosen for alteration. An hypothesis normally yields more than one prediction for which the background knowledge is not exactly the same and changing the background knowledge means that many hypotheses which were corroborated are now refuted.

According to Imre Lakatos scientists limit their choice and inspiration by following a strategy. They are committed to research programmes, which may be characterized by their hard core. The hard core consists of hypotheses which are considered irrefutable. They are protected from falsification by a protective belt of additional hypotheses, which are subject to adjustment and replacement if criticism so requires. The hard core is only affected if the programme turns from progressive into degenerating. The programme then no longer produces results that widen the theory by removing its anomalies (Lakatos, 1978, pp. 47–99).

Economics is no physics. Physics knows universal numerical parameters, whereas economics, when we formalize its theories, knows only algebraic constants which are subject to restrictions. Some writers even assume that these 'constants' are actually placeholders for what are really variables which can freely change. Paul Samuelson bases his (1948) theory on this assumption. I call this his 'parametric paradox'

(Klant, 1984, pp. 153–7). His economic theories are not pragmatically refutable.

Suppose we have the following miniature theory describing an equilibrium:

$$Y = C + I$$
$$C = (1 - s)\, Y, \qquad 0 < s < 1$$

The theory implies:

$$\frac{dY}{dI} = \frac{1}{s} > 0.$$

This is a qualitative prediction, under the condition, however, that s is a constant. If s is a variable whose change cannot be predicted, the theory implies:

$$\frac{dY}{dI} = \frac{1}{s} - \frac{Y\, ds}{s\, dI} \gtrless 0.$$

This is a tautological non-prediction.

If s is a constant, s is, in principle, measurable as to time and place. This is what econometrists do. They postulate fairly stable parameters which they estimate for a certain time–space. Their specific models are refutable. Because insufficient supplementary hypotheses are available to describe the complete situation, they use probability calculus. The principles of regression analysis belong to the econometrists' auxiliary hypotheses.

Andreas Papandreou (1958) has, however, shown in a set-theoretic analysis that a refuted specific model does not refute the basic theory. The model may be wrong, the theory may be right or wrong. This is so because an economic specific model, contrary to a physical specific model, is not an instance of the basic theory but an interpretation thereof. Not the theory, but the interpretation may be wrong.

A basic theory allows empirical investigators too much choice. They add a set of additional assumptions, m, to the specific model so that I & H & B & $m \rightarrow P$. m is determined by the investigators' translation of theoretical concepts into operationally defined concepts; their application of aggregation and disaggregation; their plugging in assumptions justifying the use of proxies; and their choice of a dynamic version of the theory by introducing time as a variable and dating the variables (which implies a choice of lags). The mathematical forms of the relations also rest upon choices, and the specific model is often augmented by hypotheses about the specific situation which are not included in the theory and the available supplementary hypotheses.

A pragmatic falsification of an economic basic theory would be possible, if it were feasible to try out all possible interpretations of a theory or, as Papandreou writes:

> The theory will be rejected if all the elements of a class of interpretations lead to a rejection of the hypothesis, which occurs in the theory, as a result of confrontation with empirical data (Papandreou, 1958, p. 135).

So far the effective procedure has not been found. Specific models which refer to a specific time–space are (pragmatically) refutable. Basic theories are not. The failure of a specific model can be attributed to the theory or to the specific assumptions of the model. Econometricians therefore generally do not test. They estimate. They describe a situation in the light of a theory without putting it to the test.

In economics the complex $H \& B$ is not falsifiable because the assumptions m have been added. Basic theories in economics can be seen as heuristic systems. They generate specific models which are refutable. They are not refutable themselves like physical theories. Physics postulates universal numerical parameters. Physical specific models are therefore instances, whereas economic specific models are interpretations.

According to Popper, systems which are irrefutable are metaphysical. They are developed in a process of critical discussion, but are not subjected to empirical tests. Their adherents consider them *plausible*, but they never can reach the stage of being corroborated. They solve problems. They are logical and do not contradict accepted truths. Popper's first and third lines of criticism apply.

Economics shows a certain similarity to metaphysics. Theoretical economists discuss the plausibility of their theories, but if they are interested in the real world they seek practical application and devise specific models. Theories which cannot be specified, such as capital theory, are sterile. Success of the refutable specific models adds to the plausibility of their theories. Because of this, economics also shows a certain similarity to physics.

It can be maintained that economics does not differ fundamentally from physics, but only gradually. The introduction of m increases the complexity that already exists due to the presence of *B*. But if it is gradual, the difference is great. In physics the specific model shows the same numerical parameters as the complex theory *H&B*; in economics they partly depend on the specific assumptions of the model. To this must be added that economics has insufficient supplementary hypotheses available and that usually also *I* is refutable. The initial condition, that is, the values of the exogenous variables, must be estimated on the basis of guesses in advance if the specific model is applied for prediction. Predictions may be wrong because the model is wrong or because the estimated values of the exogenous variables differ from the realized values.

The additional complexity of economic theories means that economics shows a higher degree of theorical pluralism than physics. It is all a matter of different logical complexity, that is, a different distribution of refutability.

PLAUSIBILITY

Analysis of the logical structure of economic theories shows that basic theories do not comply with Popper's condition of falsifiability. They are heuristic systems. If they are accepted it is because of their attributed plausibility. They can be considered seemingly true (by their adherents).

It can be maintained, of course, that physical theories are plausible too. That is so in view of the Duhem–Quine thesis; the existence of anomalies in research programmes according to Lakatos; and in general the fact that universal statements cannot be verified. Scientific theories are, however, criticizable along Popper's four lines. Economic basic theories are defective in this respect. The gap must be filled with plausible reasoning. When I speak of 'plausibility' I mean that additional activity. 'Differences make a difference', William James said. I speak of plausibility of a higher degree.

It is well worth remarking in this connection that Popper's philosophy actually must be considered to constitute a comparative static long-term metatheory. It is the description of an ideal. What happens on the time path is described by Kuhn, Lakatos and Feyerabend. Even the Dadaistic picture of the latter contains an ideal. Feyerabend sees in the activities of methodologists to maintain law and order an attempt that is harmful to *progress*:

An empiricist may regard progress as the development towards a theory whose basic assumptions have been tested. Others may see in it the development towards a logical, consistent whole of theories and hypotheses, if necessary at the expense of complete agreement with the facts (Feyerabend, 1975, p. 27).

Consistency and testing are also the ingredients of Popper's ideal. Testing in economics is affected by a gap to be plausibly filled.

Economists have adopted certain *plausibility strategies*. They see them as leading to the truth, but actually the strategies do not yield universal statements that are corroborated. They see these as evident, but actually they are not fully subjected to integral Popperian criticism. They are plausible (to their adherents) to a higher degree.

One of these strategies is that of the *realism of assumptions*. It was explicitly stated for the first time in 1691, when Roger North introduced the text of his brother Dudley with the explanation that this was for once a philosophical – that is, in the language of today, *scientific* – treatise, for in accordance with Descartes's requirement, the *Discourses upon Trade* derives the workings of the trade mechanism 'from principles undisputably true' (North [1691] 1954). The idea of the Cartesian structure of economic theories was further developed by John Stuart Mill and Nassau William Senior. Their arguments have been taken over by John Elliot Cairnes, John Neville Keynes and Lionel Robbins. I dealt elaborately with these authors in my 1984 book.

I call the above 'empirical apriorists', for they keep faith with their empiricist conscience by basing their 'principles undisputably true' on experience. According to Robbins, the generalizations of economists are ultimately based on simple facts of experience which are incontestably established (Robbins [1932] 1946, pp. 104–35). If the fundamental postulates of economics, he reasons, are true by virtue of their simplicity and immediate familiarity, then the conclusions must also be true (Klant, 1984, p. 57). 'Economic laws', Robbins wrote, 'describe inevitable implications' (Robbins [1932] 1946, p. 121). Mill called it the 'concrete-deductive method' or '*a priori* method' and the establishment of premises 'direct induction'.

There are also rationalistic apriorists. They attribute a special quality to the principles undisputably true. According to Ludwig von Mises they are Kantian synthetic judgements *a priori*, propositions which are necessarily valid and cannot be proved by any experience, just like the 'categories' of spatiality and causality (Mises, 1962, p. 56). They are essentially *forms* of experience. Economics is a branch of praxeology. It has a teleological character.

Whatever empirical and rationalistic apriorists may think of their methods of proving the truth, they do not establish the acceptability of a theory by testing the conclusions from their premises. They are describing an alternative practice of plausible reasoning which fills the gap. They are following a plausibility strategy.

Another plausibility strategy is the method of *diminishing abstraction*. The economists start with a highly idealized case and gradually diminish its simplicity and abstractness by introducing conditions which make it truer to reality. Marx's *Kapital* is a very good example, but the work of consecutive authors, too, can often be arranged in a pattern of diminishing abstraction. Progress in the natural sciences can be depicted in a similar way, but it is more restrained by the condition of continuous empirical testing than the development of separate branches of economics. There, the gradual 'concretization' by assuming more real conditions is considered in itself an increasing approximation of truth. The logical analysis of the development of the neoclassical theory of international trade by Bert Hamminga (1982) and that of the capital debate by Jack Birner (1990) are good illustrations.

Where logic and testing fall short, the *metaphor* enters. A metaphor is a figure of speech in which one thing is likened to another, different, thing by being spoken of as if it were that other. According to the philosopher David Cooper, a metaphor has no meaning, it has no truth value, but:

> Much of the interest and pleasure we feel in certain metaphors is due to the searches they send us upon ... . What makes them eminently repeatable is that they keep open lines of thought, directions in which to search (Cooper, 1986, p. 250).

It is exactly in this way that researchers use metaphors. A metaphor is a heuristic device.

Sometimes the lines of thought get closed by continuous research. 'Force' has no longer an anthropomorphic flavour, but has become a testable relationship between particles. It is a dead metaphor. A metaphor can be killed by an operational definition such as, for instance, 'price level' by 'price index number', but the theoreticians are not always prepared to adopt the inventions of the empirical researchers. 'Aggregate capital' and 'human capital' are still living metaphors.

In physics metaphors are ways of discovery. They are abandoned when the research programme comes to an end, such as, for instance, the Rutherford–Bohr model, in which the structure of an atom was likened to that of a solar system. In economics the lines of thought usually remain open. Walras's metaphor of classical mechanics is still alive (Mirowski and Cook, 1990). It changed our view, but its outcome was not a corroborated theory.

The main metaphor of the economists is that of the mechanism. Adam Smith wrote in his *Theory of Moral Sentiments*:

> Human society, when we contemplate it in a certain abstract and philo-sophical light, appears like a great, immense machine whose regular and harmonious movements produce a thousand agreeable effects (Smith [1759] 1976a, p. 316).

We are still looking with the pleasure of scholars and researchers at the huge machine. Our models describe mechanisms.

The fundamental hypotheses upon which our theories rest are idealizations *and* metaphors. The rational actors in microeconomics, deciding under conditions of perfect and imperfect competition, certainty and uncertainty, do not exist. They are stylized; that is, they are metaphors. They produce plausible results.

Here is another metaphor. In economics metaphors have a longer life than in physics. They do not change as easily into testable relations. Economics is therefore poetry to a higher degree. As Donald McCloskey rightly says: 'What is successful in economic metaphor is what is successful in poetry, and the success is analysable in similar terms' (McCloskey, 1985, p. 78).

REFLEXIVITY

One of the main foundations of economics as a plausible system is the 'realistic assumption' of rational behaviour. If a theory, however, explains how people behave rationally, you can also learn from it what you should do if you want to behave rationally. The behavioural assumptions are the axioms of a praxeology. According to Mises, it is even the only form of economics.

The use of economics as praxeology contributes to the creation of conditions that are postulated in the theory itself. Economic behaviour

is not only observed and explained by economists, but also disseminated by them. Economics is *reflexive*; there is an interaction between
theory and reality.

Methodology is reflexive too. Methodology explains the behaviour
of scientists according to rational principles. Methodology is therefore
seen by many not as a set of metatheories, but as a set of prescriptions.
We should, however, not leave out of sight its double nature. Economic
methodology is a social metascience that examines what economists
do; notably how they decide on the acceptance or rejection of theories
and hypotheses. They seek an answer to the question: how are economic theories formed and assessed? There is a great deal to be investigated in this context. I also have in mind, for instance, the analysis of
the conceptual foundations of economic theories.

For a lover of order and neatness who moreover wishes to raise the
status of his activity, the interrelated problems present an opportunity
to inflate the nomenclature. The term 'methodology' is often reserved
nowadays for problems that are considered to relate in a narrower sense
to the way in which theories are assessed. The related problems of
conceptual analysis are excluded, but taken together they are now
called to their greater glory as, for example, explicitly in Larry Laudan's
(1981, pp. 2–3) 'philosophy of science'.

I shall avail myself of the opportunity for isolation afforded me
through this. 'Methodology', then, no longer has the same meaning as
'philosophy of science' (as, for instance, formerly in Popper (1979, p.
386), when life was still simple), but indicates a part of what is so
called. I can accept that, as long as it does not lead to the confusion of
tongues which a number of newcomers to the literature of economic
methodology threaten to cause today by also employing the same word,
'methodology', as a more impressive-sounding synonym for 'method'.
This kind of elephantiasis of the word for deepening unclear ideas was
once described by Fritz Machlup as the use of language of the semi-
literate (Machlup, 1963, p. 204).

Methodology is used as a praxeology when theories are criticized
from a methodological point of view. Methodology is sometimes used
to show why economists are wrong, and some authors do not leave it at
that. They preach that we must aim at a different methodology able to
shape a more satisfactory theory. They ask, however, usually more than
methodology can do. Any praxeology has to take into consideration the
findings of the positive metatheory. The conclusions about the logical
structure of economic theories, for instance, cannot be ignored.

6.   Realism of Assumptions

REALISM IN ART AND SCIENCE

Reality cannot be reproduced. Artists and scientists are unanimous on that point. Nevertheless, they all make regular contributions to the creation of a world picture. Instead of striving for the impossible, which would imply describing infinite numbers of instances, they design patterns. They devise structures which enable us to order our experiences. Art and science are creative activities to ward off the fear of chaos and to control our environment. They provide us with the means to accentuate the world (Foss, 1971, p. 234; Goodman, 1968, p. 32).

Someone who examines the nature of these activities might be tempted to come to the conclusion that the world does not 'exist', but that we create it ourselves. To this idea not many objections need be made, as long as it is not combined with the idea that we are completely free to choose our own picture. Apparently the idea has to fulfil a number of conditions in order to be accepted. Both art and science are means of communication. Their products are subjected to collective criticism for the purpose of coming to the decision of whether they should be accepted or rejected.

Whoever assesses art makes an attempt to recognize a vision. It is a process which does not always run very smoothly. Innovators sometimes meet strong opposition, but usually it does not take very long until they can depend on a following of admirers and – as Thomas Kuhn would have to call them – of 'normal artists' who have learnt to see how the master first saw it. Picasso met the reproach that his portrait of Gertrude Stein did not resemble her at all by saying: 'Never mind, it will', and soon there were many people who could see as he did (Foss, 1971, p. 235).

However, not every attempt at creating art is rewarded by becoming an accepted vision. The number of art movements, however bewildering to the contemporary, is always small. For that reason it is equally tempting to come to the conclusion that the world does 'exist' and that we are made by it. But which of the two opposite ideas or whatever possibility in between is chosen, there will remain enough room for defending the idea that art (even abstract art) and science are always *realistic*.

It goes without saying that this is especially true for the empirical sciences, in which criticism is based on logical analysis and tests. A scientific theory may ideally be summed up in a number of axioms from which theorems may be deduced, and on the basis of which, through specification and by introducing initial conditions, predictions can be made. The observation of the events which are regarded to fulfil the initial conditions, as well as the observation of the events which have been predicted, provide grounds for rejecting or accepting the theory. If theory T is true, and the initial condition I is true, then according to the theory (assuming that the background knowledge is true) prediction P must be true: $T \rightarrow [(I \& B) \rightarrow P]$.

If we decide, after having made our observations, that I is true and P is true, this does not imply that T is true. It only means that the theory is not contradicted by the facts and that it might be accepted. If, on the other hand, we decide that I is true and P is not true, we *imply* by mentioning that decision that we have declared T false. In that case we will adjust T by introducing *ad hoc* assumptions or, if any creative innovators are around, new fundamental assumptions will be introduced so that the existing theory is renewed or even replaced by a new one.

It may take a long time for it to be decided that I is true and P not. The decision can be postponed by ignoring the results of the observations or by doubting their validity and then first wanting to find out what could be wrong. However, given the theory and given our decision that a certain falsification hypothesis has proved to be valid, the falsification of the theory is logically implied. It is quite possible that it is difficult to make the decision, and in any case Carnap's observation will hold that even existential and molecular propositions are only weakly verifiable (Carnap, 1936–7, pp. 425–7), but the fact remains that the decision based on the testing of a number of deduced propositions is at the same time a decision on the theory (or rather on the complex $T \& B$) itself.

Sometimes, however, testing is of no importance with regard to the decision to be made. If the prediction is a tautology – 'it rains or does not rain' – we do not need testing, for we know that such a proposition is always true. A theory from which only tautological predictions can be deduced cannot be falsified. The theory does not actually predict. According to Popper's falsifiability criterium, such a theory is not a scientific theory (Popper, 1959, p. 41).

We may, therefore, call a falsifiable theory *a theory with empirical content*. We may also say that an accepted theory is regarded to be scientifically *realistic*. Falsifiability is a logical property. No tests are needed to find out whether a theory can be (pragmatically) falsified. A formal analysis will be sufficient. Realism, on the other hand, is a property assigned to a theory on the basis of tests. A decision on the realism of a theory can only be made when sufficient observations have been made.

A theory consists of a number of assumptions which logically function as axioms. Through specification and by introducing initial conditions, we may deduce predictions from them. If the predictions prove to be valid we may also say that the assumptions are realistic.

REALISM IN ECONOMICS

John Stuart Mill (1844), who may be regarded as the founder of economic methodology, held the view that the realism of each fundamental assumption made by economists may be assessed by anyone by observing his environments and himself. He called this 'direct induction'. Economic phenomena are explained by deduction from evident premises. This idea of *empirical apriorism* has been quite a persistent one. It was more or less canonized in an essay published by Lionel Robbins (1932) and still influences many economists today in the way they think about economic science. *Rationalist apriorists* such as Carl Menger (1843) and Ludwig von Mises (1962), who proclaimed that the evidence of economic axioms is based on Aristotelian recognition, have come to the same conclusion: economists hold the privilege always to speak the truth as long as they listen carefully with their inner ear to '*die Stimme des Gesetzes*' (Wieser [1914] 1924, p. 12). According to Mises, who thought that economic science proved the justness of economic liberalism, only very few are still capable of doing so.

However, pure theory constructed in accordance with the prescriptions of the apriorists cannot be falsified, as it contains too few constraints and allows that structural parameters are regarded as free variables. Its predictions are tautologies. It consists of a formal system of definitions or is merely an untestable vision of the world. Its realism more resembles the realism of art than that of science.

However, there also is a school of positivist economic thinking which has gained much influence through the progress of modern economic research. One of its representatives is Milton Friedman, who holds the view that 'positive economics is, or can be, an "objective" science in precisely the same way as any of the physical sciences' (Friedman, 1953, p. 4). He says that differences of opinion among economists will be eliminated by the progress made in research. Fundamental differences in basic values about which men can ultimately only fight, will then no longer be of any importance when a decision has to be made for or against a theory.

Friedman has also caused some confusion by relating his positivist view on economics to his theory on the *realism of assumptions*. He turns Mill's theory upside down by stating that the more unrealistic its assumptions, the more significant a theory becomes: 'Truly important and significant hypotheses will be found to have assumptions that are wildly inaccurate descriptive representations of reality, and in general the more significant the theory, the more unrealistic the assumptions (in this sense)' (Friedman, 1953, p. 14). He rejects 'direct induction' as a method of proof. According to Friedman a theory is not to be judged by testing its fundamental premises, but 'by its predictive power for the class of phenomena which it is intended to "explain" (Friedman, 1953, p. 8). He holds that this is true for all empirical scientific theories, including the physical sciences.

In this way Friedman intends to put an end to the discussion of a number of economic hypotheses, one of these being the assumption that the decisions of businessmen on prices, output and investments are solely based on their wish to maximize their net returns and, therefore, to equalize marginal revenue and marginal cost. Doubts about the realism of this assumption have sometimes arisen. Some researchers have tried to test the hypothesis by actually asking businessmen about their motives and behaviour. But Friedman thinks that the negative results of such enquiries are irrelevant. It is as senseless to ask businessmen about their motives as it is to ask octogenarians how they account for their long life (Friedman, 1953, p. 31). The important issue is to find out whether, if costs and prices change, output will change in the way the theory says it will change. If the prediction is not contradicted, we no longer need to bother about the 'realism' of the hypothesis. If, on the other hand, it is contradicted, Friedman is prepared to commit himself to a paradox by stating that it may be useful to make enquiries among businessmen in order to find the reason for the deviations or to come across new hypotheses (Friedman, 1953, p. 31n).

Friedman has tried to illuminate his rather special ideas on the realism of assumptions by giving four examples, dealing with Galileo's law of falling bodies, the density of leaves around a tree, the behaviour of expert billiard players and Euclidian geometry. However, in these four examples he uses the word 'realism' in three different senses. Moreover, the four examples as well as his further ideas on the realism of assumptions, clearly show that Friedman has a somewhat blurred vision of the logical structure of empirical scientific theories.

Galileo's Law

Galileo's law of falling bodies: $ds/dt = gt$, in which s is the distance travelled, t is time, ds/dt therefore the speed, and g a constant, is only accurate for bodies falling in a vacuum. The constant acceleration on each is approximately 32 feet per second, and if t is in seconds, $s = 16t^2$. According to Friedman this law is unrealistic, for a vacuum does not exist (Friedman, 1953, p. 16). It appears that to him an unrealistic assumption means the same thing as what Ernst Mach has called an *idealization* (Mach, 1906, p. 189). An idealization cannot be tested by an experiment in which all postulated conditions are fulfilled. It sometimes is the result of a mental experiment, for instance to answer the question of what would happen if the thread of a pendulum was infinitely thin and completely inelastic. It is impossible to fulfil these conditions in a real experiment.

$C \rightarrow T$ is an idealization, when C is the ideal condition (for example, friction, air pressure and deflecting magnetic forces are zero) and T is a theory (for example, Galileo's law). A prediction can be deduced from this theory: $C \rightarrow \{T \rightarrow (I \rightarrow P)\}$, also to be written: $T \rightarrow [(C \& I) \rightarrow P]$. If the theory is true, the predicted event will take place if both the ideal condition and the initial condition are fulfilled. The theory can be tested if the ideal condition can be fulfilled by approximation by introducing supplementary hypotheses, or if the disturbing factors, independent of the measurement of P, can be assessed. If the theory can thus be successfully tested, it is regarded as scientifically realistic. It is also possible that T proves to be valid by extrapolation of the results of a great number of observations in which each time the degree of non-fulfilment of C is determined. In that case we may also call T realistic, for it is an acceptable representation of the ideal case on which a number of tested propositions are converging. It is clear that in these cases Friedman uses 'unrealistic' in the sense of 'dependent on the fulfilment of an ideal condition'.

However, this does not imply that if T deals with the behaviour of businessmen, it would not be allowed to make an enquiry among them. The theory predicts that, if they know their own motives and speak the truth, they will give certain answers. Perhaps there are reasons to reject the auxiliary axioms on the self-knowledge and the sincerity of businessmen, but that can only be done by testing a falsification hypothesis. In any case it is not right to ignore the results of an enquiry, as Friedman does, because of the fact that $C \rightarrow T$ is an idealization. According to Friedman a theory is acceptable if 'the predictions are good enough for the purpose in hand' (Friedman, 1953, p. 41). Apparently, he assumes that the ideal condition is approximately fulfilled when the theory is being applied. If that is so, we will be able to make enquiries under the same conditions.

Leaves Around a Tree

With his second example Friedman leads us to the realm of mythology. He invites us, himself being inspired by Armen A. Alchian (1950), to have a look at the density of leaves around a tree. He suggests the hypothesis that the leaves are positioned:

> As if each leaf deliberately sought to maximize the amount of sunlight it receives, given the position of its neighbors, as if it knew the physical laws determining the amount of sunlight that would be received in various positions and could move rapidly or instantaneously from any one position to any other desired and unoccupied position (Friedman, 1953, p. 19).

This is also an unrealistic assumption, Friedman says, for leaves do not know anything. They act as if they know. According to Friedman the assumption is, like all unrealistic premises, an *'as if' hypothesis*.

This is the way the Egyptians explained moon eclipses. On certain days which were known to them, a deity would send a swine into heaven to devour a piece of the moon. I would hardly call that a theory. Only very poor theories say: 'it looks as if a swine devours a piece of the moon', and 'it looks as if leaves know what leaves which cannot know do not know'. These are not explanations. The words 'as if' do not allow them to be that. They are metaphors to express surprise and to disguise a scientific lack of knowledge. Someone who says such a thing has seen a surprising relationship. He may be looking in the right direction, but he has not yet come across a theory of any real importance. He behaves more like a poet than like a scientist. As long as that is the case, we shall have to speak of a poor theory on a surprising relationship.

Friedman is wrong when he calls Galileo's law of falling bodies an 'as if' hypothesis. He is of the opinion that this law could be formulated: bodies usually fall *as if* they were dropped in a vacuum. But that is not so. The law says: bodies would fall in such and such a manner, *if* they were dropped in a vacuum. Friedman says: leaves behave *as if* they could think. He does not say: leaves would behave in such and such a manner, *if* they could think. On the contrary, he says: leaves behave in such and such a manner, although they cannot think.

It goes without saying that this is not the way to deal with thinking human beings such as businessmen. I simply cannot imagine how Friedman thinks he can compare economic theories with mythological ideas on the behaviour of leaves. All hypotheses are indeed idealizations. The assumption that businessmen maximize their returns is an idealization which is only valid under a certain ideal condition, but if someone wants to turn it into an 'as if' hypothesis, he should clearly say so. He would have to say: 'if prices and costs change, output changes as if businessmen maximized their returns', in other words, the assumption is now that in fact they do not maximize. An 'as if' hypothesis does not offer an explanation, but it rules one out.

But it all becomes rather difficult now, for in what way can the events predicted on the basis of the assumptions of businessmen acting as heavenly Egyptian swines now really be explained? We are left with a problem. The fact that the Egyptians were able to predict the shapes of the moon and even moon eclipses did not prove the acceptability of their 'hungry swine' theory. The 'as if' hypothesis can be removed with Occam's razor. We are left with a theory on prices, without a hypothesis on the behaviour of businessmen and are saying no more than that certain relationships have been noted for which no sound explanation is yet available. Predictions should be conditional. Theories should explain.

The 'as if' hypothesis of Friedman cannot be saved either by comparing it with constructs such as 'electrons' and 'ψ functions' in physics. These function as implicative axioms ensuring the consistency of a theory from which propositions are deduced which can be tested on their validity. Therefore, these theoretical concepts – for the theories concerned are accepted – may be called scientifically realistic. For instructional purposes electrons are sometimes represented *as if* they were globules. In the same way the relations between economic agents may be demonstrated by flows of water. However, the assumptions made in the theory on the behaviour of businessmen are explicit axioms which, in combination with others, may also be tested by direct observation. Unlike an electron, you can meet and watch a businessman every day.

Billiard Players

Friedman's third example, which he and L.J. Savage have used before, deals with expert billiard players. They play *as if* they know mathematics and the laws of mechanics and 'could make lightning calculations from the formulas and could then make the balls travel in the direction indicated by the formula' (Friedman and Savage, 1948, p. 298). This is, both authors say, an unrealistic assumption. But apparently they hold the view that we still need this hypothesis to predict the behaviour of billiard champions. This, of course, is not the case. A mathematician familiar with the laws of mechanics can describe for a billiard player how the latter may finish his game successfully in one turn. That, however, is a prescription and not a prediction. Usually even expert billiard players need more than one turn.

It is true, however, that, in accordance with the laws of mechanics, all successful shots of both experts and beginners will meet the same mathematically described conditions. The experts are better at it, but to predict their behaviour we need the hypothesis that they act as if they were mathematicians as little as we need the hypothesis that visitors to a restaurant know the chemics of digestive processes in order to explain their behaviour. It is sufficient to recognize what billiard players actually do: they are able to score many successive caroms, which meet the rules of the game and can be described mathematically. If we asked them about it, it would appear that they do not know mathematics but that their successful shots are based on insight in billiard situations and experience. To explain their astonishing abilities we would need the theories of a behavioural psychologist.

We might as well drop the 'as if' hypothesis, because it does not offer any explanation. Expert billiard players make shots which meet certain conditions. Businessmen also behave in a certain way. If it is true that they, like the billiard players, are not able to analyse their own behaviour, it is worth finding out what they do know about themselves and how it happens to be that they do things they do not know about. I can find no reason why it would not be allowed to test the hypothesis on the behaviour of businessmen by asking them about it. Like the billiard players, they will be quite willing to show their lack of theoretical knowledge and tell of their talents for making brilliant decisions. If, as Friedman seems to suppose, they are talented and experienced, but have no theoretical background, it should appear from their answers, analogous to the example of billiard players, that without exactly knowing why and how they are nevertheless maximizing their returns. The 'as if' part of the hypothesis is superfluous. What is left is possibly scientifically realistic and, in any case, should be tested.

Friedman and Savage use this example to justify a hypothesis on choice behaviour involving risk: 'individuals behave *as if* they calculated and compared expected utility and *as if* they knew the odds' (Friedman and Savage, 1948, p. 208). However, it seems to me that what they mean here is an idealization rather than an 'as if' hypothesis in the style of the animistic leaves theory or the hypothesis of the simple billiard players. The theory of choice gives a description of rational behaviour; that is, how a person would behave *if* he disposed of all required information and on the condition that he is not led from the straight path by a disturbing influence. The hypothesis makes sense if the degree of fulfilment of the ideal conditions can be measured or if we may assume that the disturbances follow a known probability distribution. In that case the hypothesis may be tested by observing macro behaviour. In principle, this does not exclude 'direct testing', as has been demonstrated by A.G. Papandreou (1953, 1957), K.O. May (1954), K.R. MacGrimmon and M. Toda (1968) and others, who investigated through experiments to what degree people tend to order their possibilities of choice according to a transitive relationship. Perhaps W.A. Wallis and Friedman (1942) are right when they say that such investigations are not very useful, as the experimental environment is not sufficiently representative of reality. But of course this does not make Friedman's theory on the realism of assumptions more valid. *If* adequate experiments were technically possible, and if the results were to contradict the hypothesis, it would have to be rejected. According to Friedman the results would be of no importance as long as other predictions which he calls relevant proved to be valid.

Euclidian Geometry

The fourth example supplied by Friedman is Euclidian geometry, which
he regards as an abstract model that describes reality on the basis of
unrealistic assumptions on points without dimensions and lines without
width. In fact, with this example he demonstrates that non-operational
concepts may be employed in theories. However, we should add that in
order to use such a theory for predictions, these should be testable. The
theory must be translated into observation language. If, then, the predictions are not contradicted by observations, we may rightly call the
abstract theory scientifically realistic, but once more it is not clear why
the hypothesis interpreted in observation language on the behaviour of
businessmen could not be tested by making enquiries as well.

J. Melitz rightly commented that the philosopher Ernest Nagel in his
criticism of Friedman's theory on the realism of assumptions, 'perhaps
intending to give the benefit of a doubt' paid mainly attention to
Friedman's use of 'unrealistic' in the sense of 'abstract' (Melitz, 1953,
p. 52n). This is the reason, I think, why Nagel holds the view that
'despite the inconclusiveness of the argument his conclusion is sound'
(Nagel, 1953, p. 211). However, in my opinion Friedman contradicts
himself also in the conclusions he makes. He not only defends the use
of abstract theories, but also the proposition that the results of 'direct
testing' are irrelevant. It appears, moreover, that while he tries to make
his point he uses the words 'unrealistic' in several different senses.

In his first and his last example 'unrealistic' means 'abstract', that is,
'idealized' and 'non-operational', respectively. However, in both cases
we have to do with scientifically realistic assumptions, which should be
tested in many different situations (and in the case of hypotheses on
human behaviour testing also implies making enquiries). Friedman
creates a paradoxical relationship between assumptions and predictions: predictions may be realistic, but the assumptions on which they
are based may be unrealistic. However, as E. Rotwein says: 'whenever
we consider the realism of the assumptions, we always consider what
may be called its implicit predictions' (Rotwein, 1959, p. 568). The
assumption T is unrealistic if, I being fulfilled, the prediction P is
contradicted by observations (Brunner, 1969, p. 501). This is actually
the sense in which Friedman uses 'unrealistic' in his second and third
examples, where it means 'scientifically unrealistic'; but he fails to
draw the conclusion that they are therefore superfluous. The assumptions that leaves think and billiard players know mathematics are not

proved valid by predictions based on them. Something that is superfluous does not have to be postulated. What is then left should be tested in
the usual way.

IS ECONOMICS AN OBJECTIVE SCIENCE?

In my opinion the fact that Friedman tries to introduce a theory on the
realism of assumptions into economic science has a deeper cause. For
at least a century economists have been worrying about the status of
their discipline. Confronted with the progress made by the physical
sciences, some economists such as Werner Sombart regarded themselves quite superior to all that and declared they have an insight into
matters which is unattainable for the physical scientist who refrains
from *Wesenserkenntnis* ([1929] 1950, p. 198). Others, such as T.W.
Hutchison ([1938] 1965), have taken a more humble attitude by saying
that economists have not done much more than construct a number of
formal theories without empirical content. Others, such as Vilfredo
Pareto, do not see any differences with the physical sciences (Pareto
1916, para. 69). Friedman also holds this opinion, but his manipula-
tions with his theory on the realism of assumptions make us realize that
something is the matter with economic science and particularly with
the provability of its theories.

The problem with economic theory is that it does not contain universal numerical constants. As Andreas Papandreou (1958) pointed out, an
economic theory does not describe a unique structure, but a set of
structures. Such a set or generic structure may be described by a system
of equations. The structural parameters do not have numerical values.
They function as place-holders of constants so that the system of equations, if a sufficient number of variables are supposed to be exogenous,
allows algebraic solutions. The reduced form equations then make it
possible to ascertain how the direction of changes in the endogenous
variables can be explained by the direction of autonomous changes of
exogenous variables.

Moreover, most economic theories are static theories. They describe
equilibriums. They meet Max Weber's description of 'ideal types' and
are based on simplifications and generalizations. Sometimes their
falsifiability is explicitly excluded as they are provided with non-specified *ceteris paribus* clauses. However, dynamic models may be constructed based on those general theories. They have time–spacial re-

strictions and the parameters have values that are estimated by econometric research. Papandreou calls them 'augmented models', as they are augmented with relations which do not occur in the basic theory (Papandreou, 1958, p. 139). These models, which allow conditional predictions to be made, are falsifiable. They have empirical content, and are realistic if they are accepted because of the satisfying results they produce.

The problem is, however, that usually the class of permissible interpretations of general economic theories is not adequately defined. The rejection of specific models does not provide a logical ground for rejecting the general theory, even if the latter is not insulated from the impact of empirical data by non-specified *ceteris paribus* clauses (Papandreou, 1958, p. 137). General economic theories cannot be falsified. They function as heuristic programmes and they are not accepted for their scientific realism (that is, for their predicative qualities), but for their plausibility. Even positivist economists who wish to behave as scientists may be forced to make decisions on the basis of empathy and thereby to adopt an apriorist's device.

In any case, metaphysical economists do not have to be afraid that their view of society will once be rejected on the basis of the outcome of certain tests. Friedman says that most differences on economic policy derive from different predictions based on the same theory and are not fundamental differences in basic values (Friedman, 1953, p. 5). However, different predictions are only possible if different classes of interpretations are possible. As long as it is impossible to apply an effective procedure for refuting each and every augmented theory that may be related to a general theory, economists will be able to choose from interpretations on the basis of preferences and prejudices that colour the artist's and the philosopher's visions.

7. The Slippery Transition

THE MECHANISTIC IDEAL

René Descartes, Christiaan Huygens and Isaac Newton taught mankind to see nature as a mechanism. Moral laws, John Locke had explained, are not essentially different from natural laws. The natural order of human society could thus be viewed as a system of stable relations.

Newton's method of discovery was dominated by his mechanistic ideal and it entailed mathematical treatment. He described nature as a *structure*, a composite of relations specified in terms of variables and constants. The variables are spatiotemporal magnitudes. The constants are universal numerical coefficients (such as the gravitational constant) or can be calculated from them (such as the constants in the analysis of motions under constraint). Some constants have different values for different bodies or materials, and must be ascertained in an independent manner (such as the mass of a body) (Nagel, 1968, pp. 169–70). The descriptions of such structures, called *theories*, satisfy the requirement of empirical proof. They enable us to make conditional predictions. They are 'concrete' descriptions.

David Hume made explicit, right from the subtitle of his *Treatise of Human Nature*, that he was attempting 'to introduce the experimental method of reasoning into moral subjects'. He was aware of the peculiar disadvantage of moral philosophy that precludes the possibility of controlled experiments but, he contended, we must put our trust in 'cautious observation of human life', which included introspection. 'Where experiments of this kind are judiciously collected and compared, we may hope to establish on them a science, which will not be inferior in certainty, and will be much superior to any other of human comprehension' (Hume [1739–40] 1975, pp. xviii–xix).

Most economists have hopefully followed his counsel, but it took almost two centuries before they could claim to have rendered the Newtonian mechanization of their world picture in mathematical language. The picture was not complete, though. In 1968 Gerhard Tintner had to 'concede that economics had not yet derived universal laws and constants like physics', but unperturbed by this deficiency he could state that mathematical economics and econometrics did exist, the latter being 'defined as the utilization of mathematics, economics and statistics in an effort to evaluate economic models empirically with the help of concrete data and to investigate the empirical support of certain economic theories'. Its ultimate goal is to achieve reliable predictions (Tintner, 1968, pp. 16, vii, 83).

The development of econometrics has been considered 'one contributory stream to the Keynesian revolution' (Roll, 1973, p. 499). What is Keynesian about it, however, is not necessarily Keynes's. Keynes was of the opinion that economics cannot be cultivated in the manner of physics. 'Economics is essentially a moral science and not a natural science', he wrote to Harrod. It employs introspection and judgments of value (Keynes 1973b, p. 297). 'It deals with motives, expectations and psychological uncertainties' (Keynes 1973b, p. 300). Yet he did not tell *why* in moral science, contrary to what the Scottish moralists had claimed, the method of natural science was not applicable. Harrod did not seem convinced, Keynes virtually confined himself to remarking that economists should do it differently. He wrote that, 'to convert a model into a quantitative formula is to destroy its usefulness as an instrument of thought' (Keynes 1973b, p. 299), but he did not explain this. In his introduction to the *Cambridge Economic Handbooks* he described economic theory as what seems to boil down to a form of applied logic. 'It is a method rather than a doctrine, an apparatus of the mind, a technique of thinking, which helps its possessor to draw correct conclusions'. To Harrod he wrote: 'It seems to me that economics is *a branch of logic*, a way of thinking' (Keynes, 1973b, p. 296 [my italics]). If we take these words literally, they convey that economics is merely applied logic, some kind of formal system such as geometry or decision theory, and thus without empirical content.

MARSHALLIAN INSTRUMENTALISM

Keynes's introductory text to the *Cambridge Economic Handbooks* is in letter and spirit similar to Alfred Marshall's characterization, when he called economic theory, 'not a body of concrete truth, but an engine for the discovery of concrete truth' (Marshall [1925] 1966, p. 159). Keynes quoted these words, and a large part of their context, in his biographical essay on Marshall, presenting them as the 'view that the bare bones of economic theory are not worth much in themselves and do not carry one far in the direction of useful practical conclusions' (Keynes [1933] 1972, p. 196). In the same Cantabrigian tradition, Joan Robinson labelled her contribution to price theory 'a box of tools' (Robinson, 1948, p. 3).

Marshall favoured a method which, he thought, had also been applied by Adam Smith but had been neglected by Ricardo and his followers. Economists are dealing with a world which is incessantly changing. They study facts which 'by themselves are silent' (Marshall [1925] 1966, p. 166) and 'are so complex that they generally teach nothing directly; they must be interpreted by careful reasoning and analysis' (Marshall [1890] 1961, I, p. 759n). He realized, however, that even in interpretation which takes account of variety and complexity cannot produce a concrete description of economic relations. The world is kept in constant motion by forces which have not been examined by economists.

> In this world ... every plain and simple doctrine as to the relations between cost of production, demand and value is necessarily false, and the greater the appearance of lucidity which is given to it by skilful exposition the more mischievous it is. A man is likely to be a better economist if he trusts to his common senses, and practical instincts, than if he professes to study the theory of value and is resolved to find it easy (Marshall [1890] 1961, I, p. 368).

Keynes refrained from formalizing his theories. In *A Treatise on Money* he plays extensively with identities, and in the *General Theory* he uses mathematics to make shorthand notes. Nowhere does he apply real mathematical analysis. This also seemed to be the Marshallian way of theorizing. Mathematics in Marshall's view illicitly simplifies what is too complex and too varied for formulae. The world is not so simple as to be amenable to representation in a mathematical model. He mainly used mathematics as a device for *framing* a theory, only to be preserved in appendices and footnotes (Marshall [1890] 1961, I, pp. x–xi). He also wanted to avoid esoteric argumentation accessible to specialists only. Economics has a social function. 'A missionary he remained all his life' (Keynes [1933] 1972, p. 167). Economics is meant to better the world and must, therefore, be comprehensible to anybody; businessmen in particular. 'Economics,' Marshall wrote when discussing the curriculum in which it should be taught, 'is a science of human motives

... it could not be better grouped than with the other Moral Sciences' (Marshall [1925] 1966, p. 171). In his inaugural lecture on 'The Present Position of Economics' he faced the ideas of the historical school and struggled with what Walter Eucken later called 'the great antinomy' between idiographic and nomothetic description; but notwithstanding his consequential view on the bare bones of economic theory he does not see a methodological difference between mechanics and economics. Mechanics too 'supplies a universal engine' (Marshall [1925] 1966, p. 159), he thought. Keynes's view thus differed on this point from his teacher's idea. Marshall's strappy methodology, scattered in his inaugural address and a number of places in his *Principles of Economics* leaves, just like Keynes's philosophy on this matter, some essential questions unanswered.

Marshall rejected the idea of 'political economy' as an art, preferring to cultivate 'economics', which is a positive science. His particular kind of instrumentalism and his appeal to common senses and practical instincts, however, testify to a conception of economics which, in the last resort, seems to be an art. The analysis is, in his opinion, not undertaken in an effort to produce a model which lends itself to making predictions, but to serving as a device for men with practical instincts who know the world, so that they can interpret a multiplicity of facts and choose good policies.

There is something odd in economics which makes one distrust economists, even when they are philosophizing about their trade. I will try to expose this oddity which, in my opinion, is of a logical nature, and will try to show that a particular logical feature of economic theories provides the missing explanation to Marshall's art and to Keynes's apodictic statements in his letters to Harrod. In order to arrive at this feature, we must first consider Keynes's methodology a little more closely.

THE INDUCTION PROBLEM

A Treatise on Probability (1921) is the purest theoretical and also most elaborate writing of Keynes. It is not about economics, but about logic. It does not come from Marshall, but from Johnson, Moore and Russell. He digested more literature in writing that book than he is likely to ever have read about economics. His intention was to solve the induction problem that had been set by David Hume.

Newton thought that he derived laws from facts through a process of 'analysis', that is, induction. He thought that empirical generalizations were 'deduced from the phenomena' (Noxon, 1975, p. 95). Hume showed that laws, which are generalizations about relationships between events, cannot be logical conclusions from observations of facts. They rest on assumptions about regularities. They are not the outcome of a purely rational process. They are anticipations rooted in habit, convention, convenience, instinct or passion. 'Reason is, and ought only to be the slave of the passions' (Hume [1739–40] 1975, p. 415).

John Stuart Mill, however, tried to save the idea that induction is a form of logic. He tried to justify inductive argumentation by providing the missing premises in a syllogistic form of reasoning. Applying this deductive–enthymematic approach he arrived at the conclusion that eliminative induction rests upon an assumption concerning the general constitution of nature. His Law of Universal Causation, in keeping with the Principle of Uniformity, was, however, no more than a Humean maxim subservient to habit, convention, convenience, instinct or passion.

Mill's four canons of eliminative induction, which he offered as reliable means of inference, producing new knowledge, were merely experimental methods. They cannot bring about verification, but only refutation or confirmation of hypotheses. His canons do not warrant any certainty that a right choice of hypotheses to be tested has been made. His justification of induction, based on assumptions about the constitution of nature, leads to an infinite regress. As Popper has rightly observed, Hume never accepted the full force of his own logical analysis (Popper [1963] 1965, p. 45). The ideas of causality and repetition are not the only maxims rooted in passion. All hypotheses, as Mill willy-nilly makes us realize, cannot be deduced from the phenomena. They are selected. Concealing the problem of choice, he leaves the process of discovery hidden in the clouds of passion.

The syllogism of the Method of Difference, for example, can be rendered as follows:

1. All events have a cause.
2. $A_1, A_2 \ldots A_n$ are the only events eligible to be causes of E.
3. In a number of cases it has been observed that E takes place without the occurrence of $A_2 \ldots A_n$, but never without that of A_1.

---

4. A_1 is the cause of E.

Whereas the universal proposition (1) seems to be a respectable premise because of its law-like nature, it is impossible to pin one's faith on (2). This does not define a principle of eligibility which could made the syllogism an acceptable model of sound arguments justifying induction in general as a rational procedure.

John Maynard Keynes tried to supply that general principle. He replaced (2) by the 'inductive hypothesis', that is to say the 'absolute assertion of the finiteness of the system under consideration' (Keynes [1921] 1973a, p. 289) and he cast off the Baconian belief, shared by Mill, that induction is capable of establishing a conclusion which is absolutely certain. Generalizations can be demonstrated *more or less* conclusively.

Following Jacobus Bernouilli I (1713), Laplace (1814) and J.J. Fries (1842), Keynes assumed that universal statements are more or less certain, that is, that they are *probable*, as formalized in the probability relation $a/h = P$. The inductive 'hypothesis', h, is a set of 'premises' from which the inductive 'conclusion', a, is drawn, and P is the degree of rational belief or probability (Keynes [1921] 1973a, p. 43). In other words, the probability of the general statement a supported by the set of statements h is P. If the relation between a and h is a tautology, $a/h = 1$, and $a/h = 0$ if it is contradictory. Induction, on which 'almost all empirical science rests' (Keynes [1921] 1973a, p. 241), determines the degree of probability, which in general is not measurable but must lie between both extremes.

'An inductive argument affirms, not that a certain matter of fact *is* so but that *relative to certain evidence* there is a probability in its favour' (Keynes [1921] 1973a, p. 245). This implies, according to Keynes, that 'the validity of the inductive method does not depend on the success of its predictions'. Repeated failure may supply us with new evidence. 'But the force *relative to the old evidence* is untouched' (Keynes [1921] 1973a, p. 245). 'It is a matter of logic and not of experience, what rational conclusions can be drawn from given evidence' (Keynes [1921] 1973a, p. 246).

Keynes referred here to the (supposed) validity of the inductive method, but not to the reasons for constructing theories. Theories are made to solve problems and new theories predict new events. He seemed to ignore this. He wrote:

> The peculiar virtue of prediction or predesignation is altogether imaginary. The number of instances examined and the analogy between them are the

essential points, and the question as to whether a particular 'hypothesis' happens to be propounded before or after their examination is quite irrelevant (Keynes [1921] 1973a, p. 337).

Popper took him seriously to task for this, but rather out of context. He wrote that 'if the value of a theory would be merely in its relation to its evidential basis, then it would be logically irrelevant whether the supporting evidence precedes or follows in time the invention of the theory' (Popper [1963] 1965, p. 247). That, however, is not so. A good theory should be successful in its predictions. The standpoint of inductive logic, Popper contends, makes scientific activities quite incomprehensible (Popper, 1959, p. 272). In my opinion this does not invalidate Keynes's argument. Keynes did not deal with the value of a theory. Neither was he reasoning in a Marshallian manner, and he did not have economics in mind at all. He only tried to show that induction is a rational procedure. When he mentioned predictions, it was in relation to the question of whether a hypothesis should be proposed before or after the event. It does not matter, he says.

FROM KEYNES TO POPPER

The Principle of Limited Independent Variety, as Keynes called his inductive hypothesis, implies that nature is not infinitely complex. Keynes sees in the success of modern science a strong indication of the likelihood of this premise and of the additional principle of atomism. At the end of his *Treatise*, when drawing his conclusions as to the rationality and the progress of knowledge, he writes that the practical usefulness of induction:

> can only exist if the universe of phenomena does in fact present those peculiar characteristics of atomism and limited variety which appear more and more clearly as the ultimate result to which material science is tending (Keynes [1921] 1973a, p. 468).

The number of eligible hypotheses is limited and we have a rational method to search for the best one. The eligible hypotheses have positive *a priori* probabilities dependent upon the intensions of the statements they contain. The smaller the intension of the condition Px, and the larger the intension of the conclusion Qx, the greater *a priori* probability do we attribute to the generalization $(x) (Px \rightarrow Qx)$ The *a priori* probability of 'swans are white' is smaller than that of 'swans are non-white'. The *a priori* probability of the latter generalization is smaller than that of 'birds are non-white'. The *a priori* probability of 'swans are non-swans', is nil.[1]

Some generalizations stand initially in a stronger position than others. They need different amounts of favourable evidence to support them (Keynes [1921] 1973a, p. 250). The testing of hypotheses under different conditions decides whether their probability can be increased beyond their *a priori* probability or not. Progress in science, it follows from Keynes's analysis, is brought about by testing more and more hypotheses under as great a variety of conditions as possible. The probability of non-refuted hypotheses is then increased. Because there is a finite number of hypotheses, we move into the direction of the best one. By pursuing the highest likelihood we improve our theories.

'Logic, like lyrical poetry, being no employment for the middle-aged' ([1933] 1972, p. 336), Keynes left it at that and turned into an economist. Before the publication of the *Treatise on Probability* he had written about problems of statistics (Keynes, 1983, pp. 49–237). A short review of Frank Ramsay's book in 1931 is his only further publication connected with his probability theory of induction. Its essence, Richard Braithwaite assured, was kept alive in the work of Harold Jeffreys and Rudolf Carnap, but the details have not survived (Keynes [1921] 1973a, p. xvi). Bayesian statistics has been the most fruitful of results. The concept of psycho-subjective probability developed by L.J. Savage and Bruno de Finetti is a far descendant of Keynes's logico-subjective probability.

The inductivist logicians have tried to reinforce one of his weakest spots. Keynes had introduced 'probability' as a primitive concept and did not attempt to show that 'degree of belief' satisfies the laws of probability calculus. 'On Keynes's theory', Braithwaite wrote, 'it is something of a mystery why the probability relations should be governed by probability calculus' (Keynes [1921] 1973a, p. xx). Ramsay suggested, therefore, what Richard C. Jeffrey called, 'a pragmatic analysis of belief'. 'The kind of measurement of belief with which probability is concerned is', Ramsay wrote, 'a measurement of belief *qua* basis of action' (Jeffrey, 1968, p. 166).

Braithwaite and Carnap considered the degree of belief along this line as a fair betting coefficient. According to Carnap it depends upon the degree of confirmation c (h, e), which measures the reliability of hypothesis h on the basis of the evidence e that supports it. The values of the c-function are probabilities, measurable in a simple language. 'The sociologically booming industry' of inductive logic, displaying a degenerating research programme, as Lakatos saw it (Lakatos, 1974, p. 259), has not produced that language yet. A formal inductive logic, free from assumptions about the constitution of nature, has not been constructed so far.

Karl Popper, who dropped the deductive–enthymematic approach, showed, however, how we can evade the (unsolvable) problems of probabilistic logic. Universal statements cannot be verified, but a principle of induction is superfluous. Popper replaced 'degree of belief' and 'degree of confirmation' by 'degree of corroboration', but the latter cannot be equated with mathematical probability. A theory is corroborated so long as it stands up to tests. The 'degree' thereof is an appraisal of the severity of these tests under various conditions. Popper holds that:

> science has no certainty, no rational reliability, no validity, no authority. The best we can say about it is that although it consists of our own guesses, of our own conjectures, we are doing our very best to test them: that is to say, to criticize them and refute them (Popper [1972] 1983, p. 222).

According to Popper, scientists do not aim at the highest probability. He uses the concept of 'logical probability', which is complementary to 'degree of falsifiability' and identical to Keynes's *a priori* probability (Popper, 1959, pp. 119, 271). Popper argues that scientists do not start from hypotheses with the highest *a priori* probability and do not go for hypotheses with the highest *a posteriori* probability: 'they have so far always chosen high informative content in preference to high probability, provided that the theory stood up well to its tests' (Popper, 1959, p. 363). A higher degree of falsifiability implies a greater empirical content. 'Unemployment rises to 12 per cent' is more falsifiable than 'unemployment changes' and, therefore, contains more information. Scientists, like entrepreneurs, take risks. They do not make hypotheses as *certain* as possible. 'Always choose the hypothesis which is most *ad hoc!* is an unacceptable rule' (Popper, 1959, p. 272).

Hypotheses, in Popper's view, are indeed subservient to the passions, but not only to these. The process of criticism to which hypotheses are subjected warrants the rationality and progressiveness of science. Efforts by Hanson, Kuhn, Toulmin, Lakatos, Laudan and others to specify the ideals which scientists set themselves and to describe how they did their research, led to a weakening of Popper's conditions in the modern philosophy of science. It seems, however, that where the road of the travelling philosophers bends, it is in the direction of augmented Humean maxims and not of Keynesian logical probabilism.

Keynes's theory of universal induction can at worst be interpreted as bad advice to strive for tautologies and *ad hoc* explanations. It does not bring us far, anyhow, if we are trying to find out what scientists do or ought to do. It does not offer a clue as to the difference between physics and moral science either, and does not contain a justification of Marshallian instrumentalism. But *A Treatise on Probability* also includes a theory of statistical induction, which has been at least a stepping-stone to Keynes's standpoint on econometrics.

STATISTICAL INDUCTION

Statistics deals with quantities, long-run frequencies of events, that is, chances which satisfy the Kolmogorov axioms for probability (Hacking, 1976). Universal induction consists, as implicitly shown by Mill, in testing alternative *universal* hypotheses. 'The generalisations which they assert ... claim universality, and are upset if a single exception to them can be discovered' (Keynes [1921] 1973a, p. 244). Statistical induction or inductive correlation similarly consists of testing alternative *statistical* hypotheses. Keynes assumes that 'only in the more exact sciences ... do we aim at establishing universal inductions' (Keynes [1921] 1973a, p. 244).

> If we base upon the data this and these swans are white and that swan is black, the conclusion that *most* swans are white, or that the probability of a swan's being white is such and such, then we are establishing an inductive correlation (Keynes [1921] 1973a, pp. 244–5).

If one takes into consideration that so-called induction actually consists of testing hypotheses, the field of statistical inference is even larger than Keynes assumed. When universal hypotheses are being tested, inaccuracies in observation attributable to the influence of the investigator, his instruments and his environment have usually to be taken into account. Significance tests are also then required. According to Wald they rest upon the use of decision functions under conditions of uncertainty. To reject or not to reject, that is the question to decide upon.

The last part of *A Treatise on Probability* deals with the foundations of statistical inference. Statistics, Keynes ascertained, has a descriptive and an inductive function. This union is the occasion of a great deal of confusion:

> The statistician, who is mainly interested in technical methods of his science, is less concerned to discover the precise conditions in which a description can be legimately extended by induction. He slips somewhat easily from one to the other, and having found a complete and satisfactory mode of description he may take less pains over the transitional argument, which is to permit him to use this description for the purpose of generalisation (Keynes [1921] 1973a, p. 361).

Keynes devoted a separate chapter to the 'inductive use of statistical frequencies for the determination of probability *a posteriori*' (Keynes [1921] 1973a, p. 427), which can be translated into Popperian as the 'use of statistical frequencies to corroborate hypotheses'. He shows himself to be mainly interested in the problem of the stability of correlation coefficients. Statisticians ought to limit their business, in his view, to preparing the numerical aspects of the collected data in an intelligible form. In case the investigators wish to try inductive correlation the statistician can render them a useful service by:

> Breaking up a statistical series, according to appropriate principles, into a number of sub-series, with a view of analysing and measuring, not merely the frequency of a given character over the aggregate series, but the *stability* of this frequency amongst the sub-series (Keynes [1921] 1973a, p. 428).

He discussed in this connection the dispersion theory of Wilhelm Lexis and its development by Ladislaus von Bortkiewicz. 'Though an admirer', he criticizes them, Bortkiewicz in particular, whom he calls 'like many other students of probability an eccentric, preferring algebra to earth' (Keynes [1921] 1973a, p. 441). Keynes stressed the point that a statistical analysis is inconclusive without a hypothesis about a causal connection between the quantities. 'The argument can only strengthen a pre-existing presumption; it cannot create one' (Keynes [1921] 1973a, p. 406). However, 'if we have a considerable body of pre-existing knowledge relevant to the particular inquiry, the calculation of a small number of correlation coefficients may be crucial' (Keynes [1921] 1973a, p. 467).

PROFESSOR TINBERGEN'S METHOD

Preferring earth to algebra and being aware of the dangers of slipping from description into induction, Keynes published in *The Economic Journal* of September 1939 a rather presumptuous criticism of Jan Tinbergen's pioneering work in econometrics ('Professor Tinbergen's Method' (Keynes [1930] 1973b, pp. 306–12)). The publication of this review had been preceded by an epistolary discussion from which I quoted above.

The story starts in the summer of 1938, when Keynes replied to R. Tyler of the League of Nations, who had sent him proof copies of Tinbergen's *A Method and its Application to Investment Activity* and *Business Cycles in the United States of America*. Tinbergen was temporarily attached to the Financial Section and Economic Intelligence Service (of which A. Loveday was the Director) of the Secretariat of the League of Nations. His task was to 'submit to statistical test some of the theories which have been put forward regarding the character and causes of cyclical fluctuation in business activity' (Tinbergen [1939] 1968, p. 11).

Lawrence Klein has called Keynes's review 'one of his sorriest professional performances' (Klein, 1951, p. 450). Even Keynes himself had his misgivings. To Tyler he wrote that he had the utmost difficulty in making head or tail of the two books and in a note to Richard Kahn he called their content 'a mess of unintelligible figurings' and thought it all 'hocus' (Keynes, 1973b, p. 289). But this time he must have felt himself walking on slippery ground, for to Tinbergen he wrote 'I hope you will continue your investigations' (Keynes, 1973b, p. 293). When submitting his review to his assistant editor, Austin Robinson, he was, as Donald Moggridge reports, uneasy that the review might be 'probably a waste of time' and 'not within my competence' (Moggridge, 1974, p. 60). 'The probable is the hypothesis on which it is rational for us to act' (Keynes [1921] 1973a, p. 339), but the probability of the waste of time was apparently too small this time to induce rational conduct.

Keynes displayed much ignorance and misunderstanding of what Tinbergen had done. Richard Stone blamed Keynes's character, bad health and rusty mathematics for it (Stone, 1978). Keynes's criticism was indeed rather awkward and embarrassing. On the one hand he claimed to be an authority, preferring 'the mazes of logic' to those of arithmetic, being one whose tastes in statistical theory had begun many years ago. On the other hand he showed himself unfamiliar with the logic of Tinbergen's simple arithmetic. His remarks on the 'ridiculousness' of linear relations and the 'devastating inconsistencies' on the fact that regression coefficients are widely different in various countries (relating to differently defined magnitudes, as he had failed to notice) are beside the point.

The first efforts to test business-cycle theory by making use of multiple regression analysis provoked Keynes to indulge his suspicion of statisticians and to apply indiscriminately what he had written on statistical inference, and on his favourite subject of stable correlation coefficients in particular.

> Thirty years ago I used to be occupied in examining the slippery problem of passing from statistical description to inductive generalisation in the case of simple correlation; and today in the era of multiple correlation I do not find that in this respect practice is much improved. In case Mr. Loveday or others may nurse inductive hopes, it is worth pointing out that Professor Tinbergen makes the least possible preparations for the inductive transition (Keynes, 1973b, pp. 315–16).

Keynes's review, all the same, contained a valuable core which Klein apparently failed to notice and which left Tinbergen rather at a loss in his otherwise trenchant reply (Tinbergen, 1940, pp. 141–54). Keynes wrote that econometrics must necessarily fail as a method of induction. He uses a Popperian argument *avant la lettre* (in Britain, in any case) in stating that multiple correlation analysis is no proper method of testing, because the incorrectness of an economic theory cannot be demonstrated by it:

> The method is only applicable where the economist is able to provide beforehand a correct and indubitably complete analysis of the significant factors. The method is one neither of discovery nor of criticism. It is a means of giving quantative precision to what, in qualitative terms, we know already as the result of a complete theoretical analysis (Keynes, 1973b, p. 308).

In other words, in Keynes's judgement Tinbergen did not test but estimate.

Keynes believed that statistical analysis as a means of induction must fail in economics because the condition of a constant environment is not met: 'the environment in all relevant respects, other than the fluctuations in those factors of which we take particular account, should be uniform and homogeneous over a period of time' (Keynes, 1973b, p. 316). This condition not being met, the curves discovered by the statisticians are a historical presentation but a dubious means of predicting the future.

FALSIFIABILITY OF ECONOMIC THEORIES

Economic theories describing a complex world which is liable to unpredictable 'structural' changes cannot be falsified. Keynes's philosophical remarks are perfectly apt. They are not merely applicable to testing by means of econometrics, but to all attempts to corroborate economic theories. Falsifiability as a demarcation criterion is a logical affair (Popper [1972] 1983, p. xx). An analysis of the logical structure of economic theories shows that basic theories in economics describe what Andreas Papandreou (1958) called 'generic structures', that is sets of structures. They do not contain universal numerical constants as in theories which describe unique structures.

In economics the structural parameters of a theory are often assumed to be liable to change, dependent upon unexplained changes in the environment. The real problem in economics is that the idealizations describe generic structures which permit an unlimited class of interpretations. Theories which merely yield tautological non-predictions abound in the history of economics. They may be useful as consistent systems of definitions, as boxes of tools and elastic supports to world pictures, they are irrefutable. They comply perfectly with the idea of economics as some kind of formal system, a branch of logic which enables us to talk about the world in a specific and consistent way. Their proclaimers always have a perfect alibi (Papandreou, 1958, p. 142; Archibald, 1959, p. 61), for no test can disprove their claims.

But most economists of the present day do not behave in that non-committal way. They assume that the structural parameters are 'stable', that is, more or less constant over time, at least during a certain period within a specific area. We can then try to estimate them according to place and time and can construct an econometric model containing operationally defined variables and numerical constants. Such a specific model yields predictions of events in a limited social space, such as the economy of the United States since 1867 or the port of Rotterdam since 1950, which have the form of contingent statements. Specific models are, therefore (pragmatically), falsifiable.

The trouble with specific models in economics is, however, that they are generally not proper instances (sub-relations) of basic theories which describe sets of structures. A basic theory allows the empirical investigators too much choice.

A specific model is an *interpretation* of a basic theory (possibly composed of elements from more than one basic theory). If it is empirically refuted, the basic theory is not falsified. The outcomes of the tests are not decisive; either the interpretation or the theory is false. Decisions on the acceptance or rejection of economic theories are taken in discussions of the *plausibility* of hypotheses. If a Keynesian model yields worse predictions than a monetarist one, Friedman need not be preferred to Keynes. The investigator who considers Keynes's theory more plausible and more in conformity with his 'natural order' producing 'agreeable effects' will reject his interpretation, but not the theory.

Basic theories in economics are heuristic systems. We decide upon their acceptance or rejection in a discussion on plausibility. The success and failure of the estimated empirical models support, as Tintner indicated, arguments in that discussion. Statistical analysis is a contribution to the discussion of plausibility. Newtons ideal cannot be realized but basic theories, the heuristic 'engines for discovery' are more than forms of applied logic. They are inspiring visions which tempt us again and again to draw mechanistic pictures – for that is what specific models are – of parts of the world so that we can choose a good policy.

In the letter to Harrod from which I quoted previously, Keynes wrote: 'Economics is a science of thinking in terms of models joined to the art of choosing models which are relevant to the contemporary world' (Keynes, 1973b, p. 296). He thereby characterized in fact heuristic theories describing generic structures. Their application is an art to be performed by those who, as Marshall recommended, trust their common senses and practical instincts.

NOTE

1. Elements in the set designated by the predicate P have properties which are denominated in the *intension* (meaning) of a concept. They can be specified in a definition. The *extension* (content) is the set of elements for which the defining sentence is true. If a change in extension is accompanied by a change in intension, they always take place in the opposite direction. We can, therefore, also define greater *a priori* probability as: the larger the extension of the condition Px and the smaller the extension of the conclusion Qx, the greater *a priori* probability do we attribute to the generalization $(x)\ (Px \rightarrow Qx)$. Keynes uses the term 'comprehension' for exten-

8. The Natural Order

Es ist ganz verfehlt anzunehmen, dass die Objektivität der Wissenschaft von der Objektivität des Wissenschaftlers abhängt (Karl Popper, 1972, p. 112).

SCIENCE AND ART

Do economic theories propound laws which describe how events occur, or do they contain rules showing how we must behave? It is an old question. In the 19th century, when economics was still called political economy, the practitioners compromised by that name asked themselves: are we occupied with a *science* teaching us how we do it or with an *art* teaching us how we must do it? In the introductory chapters of books devoted to the principles of political economy, they often represented themselves as research scientists, curious about the way in which the world is made up. But anyone who read on could also discover how they designed a blueprint for changing the world.

Adam Smith had left no doubt about the latter. He too had come under the spell of the idea proclaimed by John Locke: the laws of nature do not really differ from the moral laws by which man should behave and society must be ordered. They both relate to the *natural order* desired by God. Smith, impressed by Descartes and Newton, regarded society expressly as one large mechanism, the operation of which can be explained by reasoning and observing with a small number of principles; but, in line with ideas of Shaftesbury and his teacher Hutcheson, he also devoted attention to the world's beauty.

The awareness of this was based on admiration, viz. for the 'invisible chains which bind together ... disjoined objects'. Science – 'this most sublime of all the agreeable arts' – which arouses awareness of coherence, simplicity, familiarity and propriety (Reisman, 1976, pp. 45–67), introduces order into the chaos, restoring it to a 'tone of tranquillity and composure' (Smith [1795] 1980, pp. 45–6). He regarded what the mechanism produces, if we only give it a chance, as 'agreeable effects' (Smith [1759] 1976a, p. 316).

The *Wealth of Nations* is largely devoted to an explanation of the connections between economic events, but it did not stop there. Smith did not make much use of the term 'political economy', but if he did employ it, it was concerned (as in the case of his cameralistic fellow-countryman James Steuart, whom he ignored) with statesmanship:

> Political economy, considered as a branch of the science of a statesman or legislator, proposes two distinct objects, to provide a plentiful revenue or subsistence for the people, or more properly to enable them to provide such a revenue or subsistence for themselves; and secondly, to supply the state or common wealth with a revenue sufficient for the public services. It proposes to enrich both the people and the sovereign (Smith [1776] 1976b, p. 428).

Smith therefore devoted considerable attention not only to what happens in the world, but also to what has to be changed in that world for the sake of natural beauty. The principle of *laissez-faire*, which according to *philosophes* and physiocrats was part of the natural order, but which had been incompletely realized in the positive order, was for Smith, too – although he never used the *words* – a determinant of his 'obvious and simple system of natural liberty', which at the same time was a *just* system (Smith [1776] 1976b, pp. 606, 687). And yet his natural liberty was not a fact, but a desideratum. Nature in the language of the moral philosophers is something quite different from the inescapable and immutable nature that was described for them so impressively in the laws of the experimental natural philosophers. It is an *ideal*.

The nature of moral philosophy, of which Smith spoke when he considered something desirable to be 'natural', was the product of the age-old philosophy of natural law. According to Protagoras, Zeus 'sent Hermes bringing conscience and justice to mankind to be the principles of organization of cities and the bonds of friendship' (Plato, 1976, p. 322 c). After him there was no shortage of attempts to appeal to rational insight alongside or instead of divine origin: the natural order is regarded as evident by anyone who reflects. To Hugo Grotius, natural law is a purely rational construction: 'In order to be a science, law must not depend on experience, but on definitions, not on facts but on logical deductions' (Entrèves, 1970, p. 55). The philosophy of natural law in the 17th and 18th centuries is rationalistic and individualistic. Law and morals are practically the same (Entrèves, 1970, pp. 79–92). Just and good are one.

However it might be presented, there is no escaping the fact that the ideal of good relates to *possible* human behaviour. It is within the grasp of all who are prepared to heed its call, but it can also be neglected by them. There are not only ideals which we, as if motivated by an inner voice, try to live up to, but also *potential ideals*, in which fine results of behaviour are held up to us which, after careful consideration, we can decide to accept or not. Natural laws *describe* in the form of contingent statements which are true or not true. They are logically subject to refutation by empirical research. Moral laws, on the other hand, *prescribe* in the form of pronouncements without truth value. They can be neither confirmed nor refuted by empirical research (Wright, 1963, p. 2).

Today we class the 'natural' principles – prescriptions in accordance with which life is or may be lived – as *values*. They are something like *slogans*. The rules of art are dependent on values, for instance the slogan 'long live natural liberty!'[1] The natural orders of the physiocrats and that of Smith are apparently what Karl Mannheim has called 'orientations transcending reality'. In his view they may be a *Utopia*, viz. orientations 'which, when they pass over into conduct, tend to shatter, either partially or wholly, the order of things prevailing at the time'. They may also be free from such shattering tendencies. In that case they are an *ideology*, whether or not 'congruent with reality' (Mannheim [1928] 1979, p. 173). However, in both cases an image is designed which functions as an ideal and thus comprises norms for action.

A natural order evident to thinking persons, Utopian or ideological, is to be found in every classical economist. Jean-Baptiste Say, for example, proved desirous of expressly following the procedures of experimental science, but nevertheless had already given himself away in his introduction. Exactly like the laws of nature, the general laws of the political and moral sciences proceed, according to Say, from the *nature of things*. We do not devise them, but find them. They rule those people who rule others and they are never violated with impunity.[2] Like the philosophers of the natural order, Say is a victim of his own imagery. Laws of nature cannot be broken. It is possible that someone who ignores them breaks his neck, but anyone who, convinced of the immovable order of nature, proclaims how we must behave therein, is occupied with art. The rules described are not laws of nature. They relate to recommended behaviour and are dependent – if you like, by virtue of divine inspiration and rational insight – on what is considered desirable.

The law of gravitation cannot be violated by a single particle; rules of the road *can* be violated by people. Say warns that anyone who does not adhere to these may be run over. His advice in any case belongs to art, but the theory which he applies regarding the rules that are followed also proves not to be free from the apriorism that gives shape to an order of which the evident naturalness must be recognized rationally. Despite his sincere endeavour to base his theory on facts, it proves to be derived from a number of *principles which require no proof* because everyone knows them.[3]

Malthus, too, was not lacking in meddlesomeness, the basis of art. In the introduction to his *Principles of Political Economy* he states:

> One of the specific objects of the present work is to prepare some of the most important *rules of political economy for practical application*, by a frequent reference to experience, and by endeavouring to take a comprehensive view of all the causes that concur in the production of particular phenomena (Malthus [1823] 1951, p. 16; my italics).

Incidentally, I gave the title of his book in abbreviated form. It reads further: *Considered with a View to their Practical Application.*

David Ricardo, convinced as he was of the exemplariness of *his* natural order, was no less in his love of interference. He put into execution the two-fold plan of his promoter James Mill: publication of an economic work and – 'following up the written into the spoken message' – proclamation of a new doctrine of political economy in Parliament (Hutchison, 1978, p. 27). He designed a highly abstract model of production and distribution which, in the absence of specific information, had little to do with reality. Nevertheless, it proved in that barren state to give him sufficient assurance to declare in the House of Commons, with reference to a petition by weavers who had become unemployed through mechanization:

> Gentlemen ought ... to inculcate this truth on the minds of the working classes – that the value of labour, like the value of other things depended on the relative proportions of supply and demand. If the supply of labour were greater than could be employed, then the people must be miserable. But the people had the remedy in their own hands. A little forethought, a little prudence (which probably they would exert, if they were not made such machines of by the poor-laws), a little of that caution which the better

educated felt necessary to use, would enable them to improve their situation (Ricardo, 1973a, p. 303).

Ricardo described the laws of wages, rent and profits by the logical analysis of a number of principles and did not require his theory to be tested. After all – as he wrote to John McCulloch when the latter had queried the truth of his revised theory regarding unemployment as a result of mechanization – that theory was 'as demonstrable as any of the truths of geometry' (Ricardo, 1973b, p. 390). However, the result of his treatise resembled in its form a science of inescapable nature. Taking the laws into account, some things can be changed in the world (for instance by abolition of the corn laws and the poor laws, and by modification of farming methods in Ireland) but the poverty of today could have been prevented only by the poor of yesterday, viz. by their not reproducing themselves. The distressed weavers could draw the conclusion that, given the immovable order in which they lived, they might improve their personal fate and thus that of the nation only by hanging themselves. The rule of art which damned them apparently accorded with the values of the gentlemen who dined to the accompaniment of pleasant conversation at the King of Clubs, the Political Economy Club and Holland House, and who liked to see account being taken of laws accepted by them devised and 'geometrically' demonstrated by an evidently sagacious, universally respected, well-to-do and amiable man. Political economy was a science.

That science had been constructed by Ricardo in a very striking way from *idealizations*. However, that was not what was wrong with it, for no science at all can manage without 'neglective fictions' (Cohen and Nagel, 1963, p. 371). Analysis, as economists call their theoretical research, is based on considering matters in abstraction. In physics such abstractions are used by combining them with each other in order to establish resultants that describe concrete situations with sufficient accuracy. Tests and applications taking into account the complexity of reality, 'disturbances' and the inaccuracy of observations are rendered possible through this. The method of decreasing abstraction is a first step in this direction. However, Ricardo by no means led the way in this.

Science consists of an imaginary dissolution of the world into events that are not possible, followed by returning to the world and conquering it via a synthesis. Archimedes' laws concerning the ideal lever proved sufficiently usable for the construction of catapults. Galileo

Galilei showed how greatly Aristotle's inductive Method of Resolution did an injustice to the creative powers of imagination of researchers.[4] Through abstraction they devise 'pure' relations between variables, such as the free fall in a vacuum and the ideal pendulum, which are not exemplified directly in the phenomena (Losee [1972] 1980, pp. 54–5). These relations then serve as building blocks for an indirect exemplification.

The real deficiency of Ricardo's method did not consist of the voids in which he let imaginary events occur, but in the fact that he did so little about adequately reconstructing the concrete events by subsequently filling the voids. While Adam Smith, though rejecting political arithmetic, still makes an extensive call on historical experience, Ricardo seems to regard his theory as a means to prescription instead of description. Terence Hutchison rightly says of this:

> Ricardo's economics were of the most dangerous type: on the one hand extremely abstract, based on highly restrictive assumptions used largely for deductive facility, but also, on the other hand, intended to supply, *and regarded as supplying*, direct and trenchant implications, of immediate policy relevance, for the real world (Hutchison, 1978, p. 46).

On the basis of observations Ricardo is more inclined to conclude that the facts are wrong than that his 'science' is. For him idealization serves an ideal. It is not the means for ultimately arriving at reality – the positive order – but for constructing a natural order and vesting it with 'scientific' authority.

John Stuart Mill made allowance for the abstract character of economic theories and therefore called them 'hypothetical'. In one of the essays which he wrote in 1829–30 and published for the first time in 1844, he called political economy:

> The science which traces the laws of such of the phenomena of society as arise from the combined operations of mankind for the production of wealth, in so far as those phenomena are not modified by the pursuit of any other object (Mill [1844] 1974, p. 140).

The restriction contained in his definition even gave the unemployed a second chance, for evidently other goals might be pursued in society than were permitted in Ricardo's dismal science. According to Mill, distribution was open to change by structural interventions. The laws of production are inescapable, but those of distribution can be amended.

In his opinion science describes a world in which change must occur in accordance with ideals which are not expressed in the theory itself.

Incidentally, Mill seems to confront us with a paradox. In his *Logic* he made a distinction between science and art:

> The relation in which rules of art stand to doctrines of science may be thus characterized: The art proposes to itself an end to be attained, defines the end, and hands it over to science. The science receives it, considers it as a phenomenon or effect to be studied and having investigated its causes and conditions, sends it back to art with a theorem of the combinations of circumstances by which it could be produced. Art then examines these combinations of circumstances and according as any of them are not in human power pronounces the end attainable or not (Mill, 1843, VI, 12, 2).

In its dealings with science, art keeps a respectful distance, but in his definition of the science of political economy Mill nevertheless reintroduces art, for the 'operations of mankind' spoken of in the definition relate to a 'pursuit of objects'. Economists postulate laws of behaviour by assuming that individuals act in accordance with rules as they pursue their objectives. But this paradox, too, can be solved like other ones by making a distinction between object language and metalanguage. According to Mill, political economy is not an art but an investigation of the (possible) consequences of behaviour in accordance with a certain art. In economics man acts as someone who aims at maximum net returns in order to satisfy his wants, as a *Homo economicus*, a protector of his own interests and a hunter of profit. Since 1871 he has been a rational decider who weighs utility or neatly ranks preferences. Economics is not an art but examines art and, like every empirical science, yields pronouncements from which those who wish to practice art may learn how the objectives set by them can – or cannot – be attained.

The natural order, the ideal that inspires deeds, was, however, not yet banished therewith. Schumpeter has called the fundamental assumption on which neoclassical theory bases the description of the behaviour of deciders, as sociologists also do, *methodological individualism* (Schumpeter, 1908, pp. 88–9). The explanation of economic events is based on the decisions and corresponding actions of separate individuals. It has nothing to do with democracy and suffrage, and the slogan *laissez-faire* is not implied in it either. Nevertheless, it demonstrates a similarity to the ancient natural order. It is a different view of the importance of every human being in society from that which proceeds from the holistic philosophy which has its adherents among Marxists, historicists and institutionalists. It can of course be presented, as Schumpeter in fact did, as a fundamental hypothesis which is justified by logical analysis and the outcome of empirical tests. But if testing is deficient – and that is the case in economics – the opposite may also apply: methodological individualism will then contribute to justification of the theory, just as natural liberty once did.

The believer in the theory can try to advocate the *plausibility* of the fundamental assumption by, for instance, recalling that it is a fact that all individuals act and thus decide; but by doing so he does not demonstrate that this proposition contributes to a better explanation of events than, for example, the premise that individuals usually act without really deciding and that their behaviour is in fact determined by institutions. If acceptance of that hypothesis cannot be decided on by intersubjective testing either, we are left with a choice which is partly dependent on extra-scientific values, our view of man and society and thus of what can be made of the world.

If empirical argument proves inadequate, it will, for that matter, not remain such a simple choice. The decision to accept or reject a theory will then depend on a complex of properties thereof. Someone who opts for methodological individualism may, for instance, give further consideration to whether he will explain entrepreneurial behaviour by participating in what Spiro Latsis, in the style of Karl Popper and Imre Lakatos, calls the situational deterministic research programme of neoclassical microeconomics, or in the economic behaviourism of Simon, Baumol, Quandt, Cyert, March and others (Latsis, 1976a, 1976b, pp. 207–45).

If a choice has to be made between theories on the basis of preferences and prejudices, the strict separation between science and art desired by Mill has little chance. A view of man taking action implies norms. The natural order, the preferred picture of society, is then not easy to eliminate, even by those who are all in favour of the practice of economic *science*. Science that examines the consequences of art does then in any case yield potential ideals.

THE NEW NATURAL ORDER

That Locke's natural order did not disappear from economics with either the physiocrats or the classical economists is shown by the work of Léon Walras, who laid the foundations of contemporary neoclassical general equilibrium theory. He distinguishes between three forms of political economy. The first is that of pure political economy (*économie politique pure: théorie de la richesse sociale*). To him this consists of a static theory in which transactions are assumed to be subject to an unspecified process of *tâtonnement* that leads to a general equilibrium, as represented by a number of equations relating to demand, production and supply of goods and services. Prices come about through perfect competition in interdependent markets of finished goods, productive services of labour, land and capital, and of financial assets. The participants are fully informed about the prices which have come about and act in accordance with utility functions which are invariant during the process of *tâtonnement*.

Walras was aware that economic equilibrium does not occur in reality and that in the latter the conditions of his model are insufficiently satisfied: 'the Walrasian attempt to explain the market system takes place in a *cognitive, motivational and institutional vacuum*' (Albert, 1979, p. 119). His proof of existence – at least the attempt to do so – is purely mathematical, viz. of a unique solution of his system of equations. But, like Quesnay and Smith, he wanted to reform the world in terms of his ideal. He investigated not out of pure curiosity, but in order to be able to use science (Boson, 1950, p. 106). In applied political economy (*économie politique appliquée: théorie de la production de la richesse sociale*) he endeavoured to examine how the ideal could be realized as much as possible. Disturbances of his desired system ought to be avoided and countered, '*la science étant definie l'idéalisation de la réalité et l'art étant definie la réalisation de l'idéal*' (Walras [1898] 1936, p. 21; my italics). Science brings about an idealization and art realizes the ideal. Idealization functions in Walras as ideal.

To that end the necessary inroads had to be made into the principle of *laissez-faire*. Walras advocated government intervention, such as control of money creation, protection of consumers and supervision of advertising, nationalization of businesses with increasing returns to scale, supervision of railways and freight rates, a ban on speculation on the stock exchange by other than well-informed specialists, and international labour legislation. He believed that it is not possible to leave all enterprises free. On the other hand (although he was not in favour of it), he considered it quite feasible to expropriate them all, for that would not be at variance with liberty, equality, order and justice, if only the free market mechanism were to continue to exist. The operation thereof thus proves in his opinion to conform to the values of the French Revolution, and his natural order allows of variants. Market socialism is a form of Walrasian nature.

The reason why Walras wanted to see the world organized in accordance with his pure theory was that, according to him, thanks to the perfect market mechanism a maximum of utility is produced within certain limits or, as he could have put it today, that, given the circumstances, an optimum situation is realized for each individual participant in the system. Everyone aims at maximum satisfaction of wants and achieves the best position that is compatible with that of the others. On account of some *obiter dicta* of Vilfredo Pareto on maximum collective ophelimity, we today call that imaginary state of affairs 'Pareto-optimal' and a system making its achievement possible 'Pareto-efficient'. The welfare of no single individual can be increased without at least one other individual suffering a setback as a result.

Walras was convinced that by demonstrating the efficiency of his potential ideal he had supplied no proof of its justness.[5] The Pareto-optimum defines an ideal called 'efficiency', which is worth pursuing, but for the rest it has no ethical effect. It depends on a number of boundary conditions, such as the distribution of property, that are open to change and then result in a different income distribution. Each distribution of property has a different optimum.

Walras wished to see the question of a just distribution posed in 'social economics' (*économie sociale: théorie de la répartition de la richesse sociale*). His own contribution to this consisted principally of a plea for nationalization of land, in emulation of his father Auguste Walras, Hermann Heinrich Gossen and John Stuart Mill (Walras [1898] 1936, pp. 267–80), and in agreement with the demands of the Communist Manifesto. He was an advocate of consumer and producer co-operatives, by which everyone would be a capitalist and a worker at the same time, firms would be democratized and democracy would be activated. He calls himself a 'scientific socialist' in contradistinction to the Marxists, who took no account of the laws of supply and demand (Walras [1898] 1936, pp. 229–33). His socialism was responsible for the rules which he devised, taking into account the laws of the market mechanism, for realization of the ideals of efficiency and justice.

According to Wiliam Jaffé, Walras had much more drastic moralistic intentions with his pure theory (Jaffé, 1977). Donald A. Walker has rightly disputed this interpretation (Walker, 1984), but Walras's statement on the relation between science and reality is not affected by his criticism. Walker is of the opinion that Walras used the word *idéal* for 'idealization' (Walker, 1984, p. 452). However, that opinion is not supported in the cited statement. Walras considered art necessary to realize the ideal, and he therefore gave the word a normative connotation. As Jaffé mentions, Pareto was in any case not very taken with Walras's idealism. With reference to it he wrote to Pantaleoni that he did not agree that pure theory demonstrates what the facts ought to be. He considered it inadmissible to study what ought to be instead of what is.[6] In his publications, too, he evinced such empirical scientific intentions. In his opinion, pure science describes but does not prescribe.

However, our problem is not solved by the uttering of such good intentions. The thinkers may mean well, but the question of whether economics *is* science or art is not concerned with what the economists want, but with what they do and can do. Walras's example shows in any case that pure theory can be used to reform the world. It is a potential ideal, for economics is research into the consequences of art. The question remains whether the theory which is then used as an *ideal* to live by, Utopian or ideological, which may be embraced or rejected because it is regarded as attractive or not, can at the same time – as Pareto desired – be an indirectly tested *idealization*, such as Galileo's law describing free fall in a vacuum. And what is the art of which, it seems, both the applied and the social economics of Walras forms part? Does it contain a description of economic policy, for which the politicians supply the objectives and the economists a description of the means and measures? Or is the art an 'instrumental theory' based on further research because pure theory yields too little information?

The latter interpretations was proclaimed by Nassau William Senior. Upon assuming his chair at Oxford on 6 December 1826, he said:

> The science of Political Economy may be divided into two great branches, the theoretic and the practical. The first, or theoretic branch, that which explains the nature, production and distribution of wealth, will be found to rest on a very few general propositions, which are the result of observation, or consciousness, and which almost every man, as soon as he hears them, admits as familiar to his thoughts, or at least, as included in his previous knowledge. Its conclusions are also nearly as general as its premisses; – those which relate to the nature and production of wealth, are universally true: and, though those which relate to the distribution of wealth, are liable to be affected by peculiar institutions of particular countries – in the cases, for instance, of slavery, corn-laws, or poor-laws – *the natural state of things* can be laid down as the general rule, and the anomalies produced by particular disturbing causes can be afterwards accounted for. The practical

branch of the science, that of which the office is to ascertain what institutions are most favourable to wealth, is a far more arduous study. Many of its premises, indeed rest on the same evidence as those of the first branch, but it has many which depend on induction from phenomena, numerous, difficult of enumeration, and of which the real sequence often differs widely from the apparent one (Senior [1826] 1966a, pp. 7–9; my italics).

A quarter of a century later Senior came to speak again of his division into two branches in four lectures on the development and the nature of political economy. He called practical political economy an art: 'the art which points out the production and accumulation of wealth', or, more specifically: 'most conducive to that production, accumulation, and distribution of wealth, which is most favourable to the happiness of mankind' (Senior [1852] 1966b, p. 36).

Senior's Ricardo-inspired apriorism, which leads to a Cartesian structure of the theory, is characteristic of the methodology of the classical and many neoclassical economists. Senior's description of the theoretical branch of political economy thus recalls the natural order, which is assumed to be evident to anyone who reflects for a moment and examines himself and his surroundings. The practical branch, which he later calls 'art', cannot manage without inductions. Is that not empirical science *par excellence*? Apparently the practical branch is science and art at the same time.

In political economy art and science seem to merge. Moreover, it seems very much as if pure theory, which describes the 'natural state of things' functions not only as an idealization for explaining reality but, as was to find unconcealed expression in Walras, also as an ideal for changing it. The rules of art, which can be made subservient to other values than solely those of efficiency, cannot in Senior's view be drawn up without further empirical research. Despite the geometric proofs of Ricardo, he believed, for instance, that it ought to be investigated whether the poor laws caused the population of England to increase or decrease (Senior [1826] 1966a, p. 9).

John Neville Keynes advocated a different division of work. He was in favour of an independent science, in which Senior's pure theory and the empirical part of his practical theory would be combined. However, in his view science was practiced for the sake of art:

It is universally agreed that in economics the positive investigation of facts is not an end in itself, but is to be used as the basis of practical enquiry, in which ethical considerations are allowed their due weight. The question is not whether the positive enquiry shall complete as well as form the foundations of all economic discussion, but whether it shall be systematically combined with ethical and practical enquiries, or pursued in the first instance independently. The latter of these alternatives is to be preferred on grounds of scientific expediency (Keynes [1880] 1963, p. 47).

Keynes made a distinction between positive science, normative science (ethics) and art (politics). The art which is the last aim of economists depends on the normative and the positive science. The division of work was, for him, a matter of expediency. The question of whether economics, in which it is assumed that people act in accordance with certain rules, *can* be practiced as a positive science without implying normative science (that is, without the conception of a natural order which represents the conditions which the world should satisfy) does not occur to him.

Nor was the question put in the article which Lujo Brentano published in 1836. He drew attention to the disunity among economists which had increased in his days; they were governed by differing socio-political ideals and accused one another of servitude to pressure groups. The definition of a professor by Lorentz von Stein: 'someone who is of a different opinion', seemed to him excellently applicable to those occupying chairs of economics (Brentano, 1911, p. 45). In his opinion the true science teaches first 'what was and why it was so', secondly 'what is', and thirdly affords clues for the future (Brentano, 1911, pp. 709–10). Not for nothing was he a member of the historical school.

Interpretation of history opens the possibility of a natural order which – as in Karl Marx – proceeds in time. However, Brentano is convinced that research necessarily leads to objective results if only the researcher is unbiased. He therewith describes a symptom of what I call the St Anthony syndrome. This occurs among industrious social researchers who, convinced of their virtuousness, believe that they can resist all temptations. In Brentano's opinion, they must be on their guard above all against themselves; for national circumstances, membership of a social class, family circumstances in which they grew up, special individual interests and traditions, summon up for every problem associations of ideas among the researchers which threaten to divert them from their purpose (Brentano, 1911, p. 699).

With the above Brentano is demanding something inhuman which is not even necessary for the attainment of scientific objectivity. The St Anthony syndrome is curable. Without preferences and prejudices – if there is in fact a difference between the two – in other words, without ideals, no researcher can exist before, during and after his work. His view of the world cannot be an empty one. *Der Mann ohne Eigenschaften* does not exist. 'Do your research without bias' is therefore a piece of advice which will not lightly be given to a natural scientist, unless the intention is that, if he is able to maintain his theory successfully, he must make allowance for criticism. 'To attain objectivity, we cannot rely on the empty mind', writes Karl Popper, 'objectivity rests on criticism, on critical discussion, and on the critical examination of experiments' (Popper, 1975, p. 79). The objectivity of theories consists of the fact that they can be tested inter-subjectively (Popper, 1959, pp. 37–44). As a result, the suspicion arises that Brentano's requirement could proceed from the belief that it is possible for an economist to resist all criticism, if he sticks to his ideals. The disputes between professors would then be impossible to resolve.

THE VALUE JUDGEMENT CONFLICT

Lujo Brentano was an adherent of German socialism of the chair. The academic socialists expressly rejected *laissez-faire* and had combined in 1872, under the leadership of Gustav Schmoller, to form the *Verein für Sozialpolitik*. The aim of this association was to disseminate the idea of social reforms and State intervention so as to restrain the class struggle and avert the danger of revolution that had been summoned up by the advent of the social democrats.

According to Schmoller, it was wrong to derive economic laws of nature from man's rules of behaviour and to speak of a natural economic order (Schmoller, 1873, p. 52). Nevertheless, the natural order in the sense of a social ideal was not alien to him, as evidenced by what he wrote about the association's points of departure. They set themselves the aim, he stated, to go not only into the natural technical causes, but also the psychological ones. They assumed that an ethical process of development was going on. They believed in progress.[7]

Progress manifested itself to Schmoller as the gradual realization of the principle of distributive justice. The ideal of a just income distribution is, for him, the leading idea of social reform (Gehrig, 1914, p. 197). Otherwise than in the case of Walras, however, his social economics is not based on the ideal of justice in combination with a pure theory, but with historical description in which, as befits in the country of Hegel, the idea of justice being gradually realized is reflected.

The mix of ethics and science advocated by academic socialists such as Gustav Schmoller, Adolph Wagner and Georg Friedrich Knapp was opposed by a younger generation in the association, to which Max Weber, Werner Sombart and Franz Eulenberg belonged. Weber, in an article published in 1904 on the objectivity of socio-scientific and socio-political knowledge (in which a declaration of principle was made on behalf of the new editorial board of the *Archiv für Sozialwissenschaft und Sozialpolitik*, consisting of Weber, Sombart and Edgar Jaffé), argued in favour of a positive science (Weber, 1951, pp. 146–214). Five years later the value judgement conflict broke out in Vienna. Eugen von Philippovich, an adherent of the Austrian school and of *verstehende* historical research, described by his pupil Ludwig von Mises as a 'Viennese Fabian' and by his pupil Joseph Schumpeter as 'one of the greatest teachers of the period', had submitted to the annual congress of the association a lengthy paper. A contribution of Friedrich von Wieser was also discussed that same afternoon. Philippovich had tried to analyse the concept 'productivity' and in particular to give an answer to the question of how the productivity of a nation can be furthered by economic policy. In doing so he indulged in interpretations that amounted to assessments of results in the light of certain ideals, that is, concrete desirabilities with regard to the way in which production takes place and to the quality and composition of the product (Philippovich, 1910).

To judge by the verbatim report, in which frequent mention is made of emotional utterances, the discussing company must have evinced convictions firmly rooted in opposite values. The influence of German philosophers was clear to see – as it indeed already had been in Weber's article. Those philosophers had, since the end of the 19th century, through the intermediary of Hermann Lotze, come to recognize concepts such as 'justice', 'virtue' and 'beauty' not only by their own nature but also by the intension of the set of 'values'. Risieri Frondizi, in his introduction to axiology, calls this a real discovery. Henceforth a fundamental distinction was made between *being* and *value* (Frondizi, 1971, p. 3).

The influence of the philosophers was reflected in the fact that the ancient methodological problem was no longer discussed in terms of 'science' and 'art', but of 'is' (*sein*) and 'ought' (*sollen*). The latter term relates to norms, that is to say to values, subdivided into 'ought to be' (*seinsollen*) and 'ought to do' (*tunsollen*). The assertion, expressible *par excellence* in an evaluative sentence in the indicative, that a value is being satisfied more or less, is a *value judgement* or *statement of value*. The statement, expressible *par excellence* in the optative, by which a norm – that is, a *value* – is set, is not a judgement (proposition), but a *prescription*, wish or injunction. Like a value judgement, it can be justified by having recourse to values. It is, then, a *hypothetical* prescription, that is, one based on values. If it is justified in itself, in other words with recourse to *intrinsic* value, it is a *categorical* prescription (Taylor, 1961, pp. 223–39). Prescriptions and value judgements are often wrongly identified with each other.

Werner Sombart, who had opened the attack on Philippovich, posed the problem and in so doing adopted in his innocence a positivistic point of view. He declared himself in favour of the exclusion of value judgements because they are not susceptible to proof and, in his opinion, are therefore not open to discussion. As long as the scientific proof cannot be given that blondes or brunettes are prettier, he said, value judgements cannot be discussed (Verhandlungen, 1910, p. 572).

The most well thought out criticism came from Max Weber. He allied himself with Sombart. An empirical science, he said, is concerned with *Sein* and not with *Sollen*. He did not deny that formulations of problems depend on what we consider worth knowing, but that has nothing to do with the scientific discussion thereof. The question of whether such a scientific treatment exists or is capable of existence in economic research did not occur to him, however, so that he had no answer for Othmar Spann, who called the ideal types of Weber himself examples of *Seinsollen* (Verhandlungen, 1910, p. 588). It is questionable whether the young Spann, who in later life, too, never excelled in clarity, meant exactly what he said, but the identification of idealization and ideal with each other is, in any case, a normal phenomenon among economists.

The fact that in an association for social economics (in the sense of Walras) *Seinsollen* was argued against was not without irony, but there was still more reason for surprise. After all, theoretical explanations in which value-freedom is advocated cannot themselves manage without values. Both Sombart and Weber reasoned on the basis of hypothetical prescriptions that do not allow of the mixing of science and art. Value-freedom itself is a value. By adhering to this they *demanded* research without value judgements. By arguing about the use of that desideratum based on value judgements they showed that it is quite definitely possible to discuss blondes and brunettes in a reasonable manner, even if no empirical proof can be supplied.

By debating the art of science they were, of course, aiming at a consensus so that henceforth the practitioners of the social sciences would do their research in value-freedom. In that they did not really differ fundamentally from Schmoller. For he trusted that the academic socialists would be able to count on decent people in the same nation and the same cultural period being in agreement with one another on the most important values (Schmoller, 1911, pp. 494–5). After all, doctors, after their physiological research, can conclude without scientific loss of face that smoking must be discouraged. There is broad agreement on the value of health.

However, it would testify to a misunderstanding of their intentions if it were thought that Sombart and Weber wished to abstain from political statements. If I may paraphrase their points of view, they merely declared that they were opposed to the decision to accept or reject theories – and when all is said and done these are necessary for practising art – being taken on the strength of value judgements. They were also against a theory containing prescriptions. Theories must be objective and positive.

In Sombart's opinion a theory had to be proved 'scientifically'. In the opinion of Weber this implied that values and value judgements may in fact be the subject of research and determine the choice of problem and the formation of concepts, but that the theory itself does not set norms. There are not scientifically provable ideals (Weber, 1951, p. 585). An empirical science cannot teach anyone what he must do, but only what he can and sometimes what he wants to do (Weber, 1951, p. 151).

In his opposition to 'ethical science' Weber thus emphasized an implication of the objectivity that he desired. In the final analysis, prescriptions can be justified only by having recourse to values. However, a theory must be proved 'scientifically', that is, objectively on the strength of facts. An objective theory is therefore of necessity non-normative, that is, positive. It contains no prescriptions. Nor does it contain value judgements. 'The thesis of "value-freedom", as W.G. Runciman summarizes Weber's view, 'is ... about the irrelevance to the validity of scientific hypotheses of the standards by which the social scientist himself judges human conduct' (Runciman, 1972, p. 59). English authors such as Robbins ([1932] 1946, p. 90), Hutchison (1964, p. 55) and Blaug (1980, p. 134), rightly identify *Wertfreiheit* with objectivity. Empirical science pursues an objective description of what is happening.

Weber was aware that objectivity is itself a value that is propounded by a methodological prescription. It is an ideal that inspires theorists, but it is not always attained. On behalf of the editors of the *Archiv*, he even acknowledged that personal philosophies of life always tend to play a part in the social sciences. They obscure the discussion. They influence the assessment of causal relations. Even the editors and contributors of the journal, he affirmed, were only human. Nevertheless, he was of the opinion that there was a considerable distance between this confession of human frailty and belief in an 'ethical' economic science that must produce norms.[8]

Apparently he also was of the opinion that 'scientific' or 'objective' research is the same as research without prejudices. According to Popper that is impossible, because an 'empty mind' cannot exist. In Weber's view, however, it is simply a question of human frailty that can be overcome. He, too, suffers from the St Anthony syndrome. According to Popper, an empty mind is not necessary at all. Objective research is based on inter-subjective testing in accordance with methodological conventions which leads to a consensus. Weber seems to adopt a phenomenological point of view. Apparently, to him the empty mind is a methodological ideal.

The way to ethical science might in that case, however, be shorter than he presumed. A theory which, as a result of human frailty, is based on a philosophy of life, gives anyone desirous of applying it to achieve his objectives answers coloured by that philosophy of life. The theory may then seem positive, just like the theory according to which the eyes of the all-seeing Argus were transformed into markings on peacock tails. However, as a result of the way in which it has been assessed and accepted it conveys a message which also could be expressed in the form of an explicitly normative theory. The indicative in which it is framed is a disguised optative.

The sensitivity of economic theory to the human frailty pointed to by Weber indicates that evidently putting economic theories to the proof of inter-subjective testing fails. Sombart and Weber realized that there is something special about the provability of theories of the social sciences compared to those of the natural sciences. If both categories could be objectively demonstrated in the same way, there would never have been a value judgement conflict. Sombart and Weber saw a fundamental difference. They complicated their metatheory considerably by the distinction which they made in the style of Wilhelm Dilthey, Heinrich Rickert and Wilhelm Windelband between the natural sciences and the cultural sciences and between nomographic and idiographic science. They postulated the ideal of the value-freedom of all science, but saw a difference in the knowledge furnished by theories of the natural sciences and those of the cultural sciences. For, according to Sombart, the cultural sciences, of which economics is one, furnish essential knowledge (*Wesenserkenntnis*), an insight into the necessity which is not derived from experience and which, thanks to *Verstehen*, causes us to see the significance of the phenomena. This makes it difficult to understand what he must have meant in Vienna by 'scientific proof'.

Max Weber, however, was somewhat less receptive to the hermeneutic philosophy. To him *Verstehen* is a necessary but incomplete condition for accepting a socio-scientific theory. Identification with the acting persons and their culture strengthens the plausibility, or what he calls the '*qualitative Evidenz*' of a social theory, but this must be checked by the usual methods of 'causal imputation' (Weber, 1951, p. 428). If we assume that the customs in the social sciences are the same on this point as in the natural sciences, the value-freedom of all science would then be explicable.

But Weber proceeds from premises that undermine his own thesis of general value-freedom. He quite incorrectly assumes that only in the social sciences is use made of idealizations. He derived the term *Idealtypus* from Georg Jellinek, the legal philosopher, and attached to it the meaning which, according to Runciman (1972, p. 9), he must have found in Georg Simmel (who in his *Philosophie des Geldes* tried to reproduce an ideal construction (Simmel [1900] 1907, VIII). Ideal constructions, according to Weber, indicate how a certain form of human action would end if it were directed solely at one economic target (Weber, 1951, p. 50). Neither this definition nor its variants which are to be found in his writings are startling to a natural scientist. According to Ernst Mach, all universal physical concepts and laws are in the form of idealizations (Mach, 1906, pp. 192–193).

However, Weber distances himself from the natural sciences. In Mach's view, facts, however complicated, are reconstructed by a synthetic combination of idealizations. In Weber, on the other hand, an idealization has only a heuristic function. It has been brought about by abstraction, and is not a hypothesis but a guideline for the formation of hypotheses to explain concrete events (Weber, 1951, p. 190). In my opinion, Weber thus correctly characterizes general economic theories. Basic theories are heuristic systems with which specific models can be designed to explain concrete events.

Yet Weber's metatheory of ideal types has a poor foundation. Not only does he fail to see that idealizations also occur in the natural sciences; he also ignores the fact that concrete events can be explained precisely by laws in the form of idealizations. Weber is of the opinion that only the social sciences are faced with the problem of the reconstruction of unique, non-repeatable happenings. However, the facts that Mach was talking about also include historical ones. Today we even have an explanation of what happened in the first non-repeatable ten seconds of the universe. Of course, a synthesis of idealizations does not represent the *complete* reality, any more than does the explanation of the selected aspects of events that Weber calls 'unique concrete social phenomena'. Indeed, that is impossible, but there is no reason for assuming, as Weber does, that economic theories cannot describe laws purely and simply because they do not explain concrete events. If no laws can be found in economics, that must be due to something else.

Walras's pure theory, for instance, is to Weber an idealization that provides indications for the interpretation of concrete events. His requirement of 'checking by causal imputation' – dare I say, testing? – is then applicable to a specific interpretation of this kind. But then the question arises: is the idealization not being tested at the same time by this? That could, in fact, be the case if ideal types contain sufficient restrictions with regard to admissible interpretations to make them falsifiable. But then they would describe a general behavioural structure which quite definitely may be called regular. They would describe laws. If, on the other hand, they are not falsifiable, it is possible that they are so formulated that they do in fact answer Weber's characterization, and function as heuristic theories for forming specific testable models. Since in that case the ideal types cannot be put to the proof by severe testing, the speculative decision to accept them nevertheless as guidelines can be taken on the basis of extra-scientific value judgements. Weber's thesis of value-freedom is, therefore, at variance with his view on ideal types.

Weber's philosophy implies that pure theories cannot be objective. His ideal types are not falsifiable. Since, moreover, as he acknowledges, philosophies of life happen to play a part, they cannot really be value-free. True, they can be taken for positive, because norms are not explicitly set in them but, like myths, they are accepted on the strength of an assessment in accordance with extra-scientific values. By utilizing Weber's misplaced apology on account of human frailty, one may continue improperly to call them 'value-free', because the theories that have come about in that way do not contain explicit prescriptions. If, however, as Mill wanted, 'art hands its end over to science', it receives in return a non-objective theorem which is dependent on value judgements that, in Weber's view, are irrelevant in science to the decision of whether to accept or reject.

In accordance with Hume's law, '*is* judgements' cannot imply prescriptions. *Ought* does not follow from *is*. Prescriptions in which norms are set are justified by recourse to values. They can, it is true, be derived from a conjunction of prescriptions and *is* judgements. However, non-objective ideological pronouncements, as meant by Weber, are not pure *is* judgements. They are based in part on value judgements. The facts are examined in the light of ideas about a natural, that is, attractive order. If a non-objective theory of this kind is to be called 'value-free', Schmoller's ethical theory of just distribution will have to be taken as value-free. After all, that theory, too, can be reproduced without explicit prescriptions. 'A value judgment may be found without being uttered in an evaluation sentence' (Taylor, 1961, p. 3). It is possible to describe evaluatively and to evaluate descriptively. If art makes an appeal to Schmoller's 'positive' science, it promptly receives an ethical reply, but not from Schmoller alone.

Just as *ought* does not follow from *is*, *is* does not follow from *ought*. What should be objective or value-free in accordance with the methodological norm is not so if it is not satisfied because of whatever weakness. For clarity's sake it would also be better if we never spoke again of *value-freedom*, but simply of *objectivity* for, as Weber himself clearly realized in his 1904 article, that norm forms the problem proper.

If philosophies of life always interfere with research, it will not be possible anyway to keep them completely away in the case of testable idealizations either. For, because we require a set of abstract laws to explain a concrete situation and to interpret our observations of that situation, hypotheses cannot be independently tested. The one theory depends on the other.

However, Duhem–Quine's holistic thesis does not exclude the possibility that researchers, by making alternating attempts with different combinations of hypotheses, may arrive by testing at a pragmatic decision as to what they will accept and what they will reject. But the conditions of the static metatheory of naive falsificationism, which completely excludes arbitrariness and speculation, are never satisfied. They apply a partial equilibrium analysis. Corroborations are based on guesses. Research is always on the go. It is, as Otto Neurath said, a ship which, while already sailing, is built with means available at sea. It is hampered by unsolved problems, contradictions, hiatures, faulty con-

structions, errors and failures. It is never in a state of general equilibrium which offers an opportunity for a unique solution and forges
Quine's 'corporate body' into perfect unity.

In recent years Thomas Kuhn, Imre Lakatos, Paul Feyerabend, *et al.*
have made us aware that every branch of science has its traditions,
paradigms and systems of concepts that may be interpreted as so many
'prejudices' which for a long time are not made the subject of discussion. It is possible to evade the falsification of certain hypotheses and
to follow strategies by which hard cores of hypotheses are spared. As a
result, even the natural sciences are partly dependent on preconceived
views and habits of thought. The way in which we wish to see the
world has an effect on how it looks. The belief in hypotheses is not
determined solely by the recent results of research, but also by the faith
that one has – rightly or wrongly – in future results.

According to Stephen Toulmin, we proceed in physics, too, from a
preconceived natural order which remains unaffected in critical discussion. In his opinion Newton's law of inertia is part of the ideal of the
natural order which cannot be demonstrated empirically. According to
Toulmin, real laws describe deviations from the natural order. Snell's
law of the refraction of light depends on the unprovable natural-order
principle that light travels in a straight line (Toulmin [1953] 1960, pp.
57–104). Hypotheses cannot be falsified without assuming that the
principles of the natural order are true.

As Karl Popper has argued, the empirical basis of science therefore
has nothing 'absolute' about it. Theories are built in a swamp on piles
which can be lengthened, but which will never reach hard ground
(Popper, 1959, p. 111). Nevertheless, we assiduously devote ourselves
in empirical science to testing theories by means of experiments, systematic observations and practical applications. We thus scan possibilities by the assessment of alternative hypotheses in varying combinations which are falsifiable *at choice* if, for that purpose, we regard the
remaining supplementary hypotheses and auxiliary hypotheses each
time as true. For in testing we decide on logical grounds: if the statements that we make with reference to observations are contradictory to
the propositions that we are testing, these are in principle falsified,
which may qualify them for rejection and in any case make a reorgani-
zation of Quine's 'corporate body' necessary. Our predictive successes
and the staggering triumphs of technical application show what imposing structures can be erected right in the swamp of nature.

In the natural sciences central ideas can be used to continue to *see* the world in a certain way. In the social sciences, in which the consequences of art are investigated, they are, however, also used to *change* the world. The ideas then become ideals, that is to say values. For the social world is a changing system which we make ourselves. It is inevitable that the view of the structure or of the process is at the same time an idea about what can be done with it. In his faith in the possibility of 'causal imputation' without speculation, Weber has not shown us how the mix of idealization, idea and ideal desired by Othmar Spann can be avoided in order to realize the ideal of a rightly value-free social science.

The value judgement conflict yielded a large number of publications, especially in Germany, by both the *Wertiker* and the *Wertfreien* (Weber and Topitsch, 1952). The former succeeded in involving in the conflict the philosophy of the day, such as that of Edmund Husserl. However, they made little impression on the mainstream economists. Political economy had in the meantime become economics, or, better still, *economic science*. The principles of value-freedom that had been proclaimed by the *verstehende* sociologist, Max Weber, were well received by the neoclassical economists. However, his related philosophy of the heuristic ideal types did not take root. The metatheory of value-freedom, purged of hermeneutics, was taken for granted, the problems of provability, which were sensed but not solved by Weber, were overlooked.

Lionel Robbins even regarded the matter so simplistically that, from the premise that economists pronounce no value judgements on the value judgements of economic agents, he deduced that economic analysis is value-free in the sense of Weber (Robbins [1932] 1946, pp. 90–91). In his well-known essay on the nature and significance of economic science, he drew the picture willy-nilly of a purely formal theory. A pure theory which, as he sees it, is based on a few obvious principles can hardly be different. However, in a later publication he concedes that hypotheses that must be tested are added to the empirically empty pure theory (Robbins, 1938, p. 346).

That it might be impossible to decide objectively on such a theory was no more a problem to Robbins than to Fritz Machlup, who in 1969 wrote in all simplicity about the problems of value-freedom that: '[they] were authoritatively treated and definitely resolved by Max Weber sixty years ago' (Machlup, 1969, p. 116). In probably the most widespread view among economists, the objectivity of research is guaranteed by the 'analysis' which takes place without value judgements and values (except the methodological ones) being involved.

According to Schumpeter, analysis consists of taking note of facts, forming concepts, positing hypotheses and applying logic. However, he distinguished two phases. One starts with a pre-scientific *vision* of presumptive relationships that can be ideologically influenced. Unlike Brentano, he believed that prejudice can be a condition for inspiration. However, *analysis* next takes place, through which the vision, if it does not prove tenable, is discarded or converted into a theory from which the ideological element has been eliminated (Schumpeter, 1949, pp. 345–59).

> Factual work and 'theoretical' work, in an endless relation of give and take, naturally testing one another, and setting new tasks for each other, will eventually produce *scientific models*, the provisional joint products of their interaction with the surviving elements of the original vision, to which increasingly more rigorous standards of consistency and adequacy will be applied (Schumpeter, 1954, p. 42).

Schumpeter acknowledges that:

> In economics, and still more in other social sciences, [the] sphere of the strictly provable is limited in that there are always fringe ends of things that are matters of personal experience and impression from which it is practically impossible to drive ideology or for that matter conscious dishonesty, completely (Schumpeter, 1954, p. 43).

Prejudice proves to be not entirely harmless after all, because conviction blinds and, as Schumpeter notes: 'The first thing a man will do for his ideals, is lie' (Schumpeter, 1954, p. 43n). Not everyone is a St Anthony. Ideological remnants thus are almost inevitably lodged in every theory, on account of a form of Weberian human frailty, viz. the stubborn belief of the researchers. However, Schumpeter proves to be of the opinion that a theory is nevertheless demonstrably true or not true. He believes that the truth or untruth is seen by anyone who is completely open to scientific criticism. Evidently he assumes that there are only two possible answers to the question of whether a statement is true: 'Yes' or 'No'. He forgets a third possibility: 'The question is not decidable'. In the last case the way remains free for the convinced to maintain their theses fearlessly and without lying.

THE POSITIVISM CONFLICT

The life expectancy of a metatheory of the heuristic ideal types was not great in an environment in which economists increasingly felt that they had to behave like natural scientists. They concentrated on making formalized theories and testing them by statistical analysis. Their pretensions are often called 'positivistic', which is not of benefit to the clarity of the philosophical discussion. In 1944/45 they had already received critical-rationalistic recognition by Karl Popper, when he published what became *The Poverty of Historicism* as a series of articles in *Economica*.

In Popper's view the method of the social sciences ought to be a 'technological approach', imposing 'a discipline on our speculative inclinations' and forcing us 'to submit our theories to definite standards, such as standards of clarity and practical testability'. Perhaps we owe it to the intercession of Friedrich von Hayek, but Popper showed great respect for economics. He recommended social scientists not to look further than their Galileo or their Pasteur, but added in a footnote: 'It must be admitted, however, that mathematical economics shows that one social science at least has gone through its Newtonian revolution' (Popper, 1957, pp. 59–60). The *pretensions* of the economists were indeed Newtonian, but were their deeds too? Popper did not go into that question.

In the same work he drew attention to what he regarded as 'a really fundamental similarity between the natural and the social sciences' by pointing to 'the existence of sociological laws or hypotheses which are analogous to the laws or hypotheses of the natural sciences' (Popper, 1957, p. 62). Strangely enough, in so doing he brought forward only the similar formulation of hypotheses which in both cases renders possible logical transformations into corresponding 'technological corrolaries': $p \rightarrow q$ is equivalent to $\neg(p \, \& \, \neg q)$. 'Swans are white' is equivalent to: 'You cannot have non-white swans'. Popper devoted no attention to the question of whether, for instance, the universal statement in technological form: 'You cannot have full employment without inflation' is also falsifiable. Apparently he assumed that the hypotheses of the social sciences satisfy the same conditions of his logical demarcation criterion as those of the natural sciences.

Popper believed that he could also demonstrate the unity of methods with an example from Hayek in which the latter represents an economist as a physicist who, through direct observation, knows the inside of atoms, but has only a limited knowledge of the complex outside situation and therefore is rarely capable of predicting the precise outcomes of particular situations, 'although they might be *disproved* by the observation of events which according to his theory are impossible' (Hayek [1955] 1964, pp. 41–2; Popper, 1957, pp. 136–7). However, Popper concluded his concurring argument by acknowledging that economists have fundamental difficulties connected with the application of methods of measurement:

> In physics ... the parameters of our equations can, in principle, be reduced to a small number of natural constants – a reduction which has been successfully carried out in many important cases. This is not so in economics; here our parameters are themselves in the most important cases quickly changing variables. This clearly reduces the significance, interpretability and testability of measurements (Popper, 1957, p. 143).

Parameters that are variable? Popper refers in a footnote to Lionel Robbins (Popper, 1957, p. 143n). He, too, failed to see that parameters that are variables of which the changes cannot be predicted turn the relations into definitions. The testability is in that case indeed reduced, namely to nil. The outcome then cannot be disproved.

In 1961 Popper gave a paper: *Die Logik der Sozialwissenschaften* in Tübingen at a meeting of the *Gesellschaft für Soziologie* where it came to an open clash of opinions of dialecticians and critical rationalists. In that paper, too, he dealt rather carelessly with the requirement which he had clearly stated for the first time in 1955 in his *Logik der Forschung*: the statements of empirical science must be *conclusively decidable* viz. refutable by experience (Popper, 1959, pp. 40–41). In Tübingen, in the den of the socio-critical lion, he calls his own point of view 'criticistic'. Criticism should consist in attempts at refutation (Popper 1972, p. 106), but he makes no mention of the requirement that social theories, to be criticized, must be empirically refutable. In Popper's language, criticizing includes testing, but he did not tell that to his audience, nor did he show he was aware of the fact that testing constitutes a sore spot in the social sciences (anyway in economics). The words 'falsify' and 'test' to not appear in the paper.

'Criticism' consists in Popper of 'attempted refutations' (Popper [1972] 1983, p. 20). Philosophical theories, although irrefutable, are also subjected to it for:

Every *rational* theory, no matter whether scientific or philosophical is rational in so far as it tries to *solve certain problems* ... Now if we look upon a theory as a proposed solution to a set of problems, the theory immediately lends itself to critical discussion (Popper [1963] 1965, p. 199).

I call a critical discussion of such theories, which can be confirmed but cannot be refuted by experience (that is, which are not testable), a rational discussion on their *plausibility*, meaning the same as what Popper calls 'to assess an irrefutable theory rationally' (Popper [1963] 1965, p. 198). The assessment serves to justify acceptance or rejection of such a theory, that is, of a choice which cannot be based exclusively on empirical scientific values. If the logical conditions of falsifiability, about which Popper is silent in his paper, should not be satisfied, economics must be regarded as a form of philosophy, with the then inevitable differing schools of thought. Their adherents try to convince others of the plausibility of their point of view.

According to Popper: 'The main task of the social sciences ... is to trace the unintended social repercussions of intentional human actions' (Popper [1963] 1965, p. 342). It is also:

The task of social theory ... to construct and to analyse ... models carefully in descriptive or nominalist terms, that is to say, *in terms of individuals*, of their attitudes, expectations, relations etc. – a postulate which may be called 'methodological individualism (Popper, 1957, p. 136).[9]

Here the method of *situational logic* is applied, which Popper presents in *The Poverty of Historicism* as a method for historians (Popper, 1957, p. 147–52) and in his Tübingen paper as the result of logical examination of economic methods that is applicable to all the social sciences (Popper, 1972, p. 120). With this he has the same in mind as Max Weber, to whom sociological knowledge is acquired by application of the ideal type of *Zweckrationalität*. It is a method that excludes non-testable psychological explanations and thus is called by Popper 'objective *Verstehen*'. The assumptions concerning *Homo economicus* or the decision theories which well-balanced individuals equipped with preference schemes and considerable knowledge are assumed to apply, are in the service of that objective understanding.

However, Weber–Popper's objective understanding cannot guarantee objectivity of the theory. If, as a result of the parameter paradox, theories are not testable and thus susceptible only to a rational discussion of their plausibility, it is conceivable that a situational analysis is extended by other means, equally lacking in real objectivity, or even replaced by them. In that case application of situational logic is not a methodological, but a theoretical problem, as in Spiro Latsis, who regards situational determinism as characteristic of a separate research programme, viz. that of the neoclassical theory of the firm (Latsis, 1976a, p. 16–18).

Methodological individualism, situational logic and the task of detecting unintended social repercussions of individual action[10] seem to be based on a choice which is bound up with a view of man, society and history. As regards Popper, he did not leave us in doubt about that. He also proclaimed a normative social theory. His natural order of the Open Society which, in his opinion has been most realized in the existing 'Society of the Atlantic Community' (Popper [1963] 1965, p. 369), is a problem-solving organization in which (in accordance with Popper's neo-Darwinian interpretation of evolution) piecemeal moderate social engineering and planning are utilized for the gradual lessening of misery by trial and error, on condition of a liberal democracy in which tolerance and freedom exist, reason is preferred to violence and the State is a necessary evil. That world must be made and maintained:

> We shall do it much better as we become more fully aware of the fact that progress rests with us, with our watchfulness, with our efforts, with the clarity of our conception of our ends, and with the realism[11] of their choice (Popper [1945] 1966, II, p. 280).

However, his view of objectivity is less easy to reconcile with his choice of the most attractive society. Just as over half a century before in Vienna, where the *Werturteilstreit* broke out, in Tübingen, where the *Positivismusstreit* was waged, value-freedom came up for discussion. Popper again emphasized that the objectivity of science does not consist of the objectivity of the scientist, but in that of the method. Objectivity is not an individual matter for the researcher, but a social matter with mutual criticism, with a friendly inimical division of work and with co-operation and opposition at the same time (Popper, 1972, p. 112). The objective and value-free scientist, said Popper, is not the ideal scientist. Passion is essential, certainly in pure science.[12] However, he thus immediately states the condition of dependence on values. Friendship and passions guarantee that extra-scientific values are respected if the scientific values cannot be sufficiently complied with.

Once again Popper makes no mention of falsifiability as a condition, which results in there also sounding in the debate the voice which, as

Kant puts it, makes nature's answer heard (Kant [1781] 1956, p. 23). If only logic, and not at the same time empirical testing, forces mutual criticism in the direction of a consensus, a gap is left for extra-scientific values that may lead in various directions. Objectivity is a property of the empirical scientific method and not of its users, indeed. Objectivity is not a property of a non-empirical scientific method like that of philosophy. Precisely because the objectivity of science does not depend on the objectivity of the scientist, the social sciences are not value-free.

In the Tübingen paper, Popper incidentally makes a statement which betrays the fact that he too sees objectivity threatened by extra-scientific values. He regards it as a task of criticism to purge the truth problems from extra-scientific values. According to him, that does not always prove successful, but remains a constant task. The purity of pure science is an ideal, he says, which is presumably unattainable, but for which criticism persistently struggles and must struggle.[13] So the St Anthony syndrome after all? It is a somewhat disconcerting conclusion after he had promised his audience the solution of the so-called problems of value-freedom in a freer way than usually happens (Popper, 1972, p. 113). In fact we are concerned here with the same solution as that of Weber and Schumpeter, which had caused the mainstream economists to be satisfied with themselves. Criticism, Popper believed, must expose the mixing of values (Popper, 1972, p. 115). But *awareness of values*, also advocated by Gunnar Myrdal (1970, pp. 55–6), however greatly it is worth pursuing, does not eliminate any values, but converts the plausibility discussion into a critical discussion of the implicit ideals. Dependence on values is clarified by it.

However, Popper's formulation, even more clearly than that of Weber and Schumpeter, can preserve us from illusions about value-freedom. Objectivity is a presumably unattainable ideal, Popper says. Evidently he considers it unattained so far. Therefore, the social sciences *are not* value-free. The scientist in the social sciences, however virtuous he might be, could on account of the absence of testability, and driven by his passions, attend to a considerable deviation from the ideal pursued.

POLITICAL ECONOMY

The idealizations that are applied in economic research fail to reconstruct concrete events by synthetic combination in accordance with

Mach's wish. This is clear to see when we are concerned with a formalized general theory which describes a set of relations, that is, a structure, by means of a number of equations. In these equations no universal numerical constants occur. They do not represent unique structures, but sets of structures. An exact imputation is therefore impossible.

Even if, contrary to what Popper supposed but in agreement with present practice, stability of the structural parameters is assumed, exact imputation is not possible. The theory is too general for that. Moreover, it is static and, if it is dynamic it is too strongly stylized. It then allows of so many dynamic interpretations that acknowledgement of the failure of testable empirical applications does not logically compel amendment or rejection of the general theory. 'The conclusions of Political Economy ... are only true under certain suppositions, in which more than general causes – causes common to the whole class of cases under consideration – are taken into account', declared John Stuart Mill ([1844] 1974, p. 149), and Neville Keynes wrote in accordance with a widespread view of political economy: 'its laws are statements of tendencies only' (Keynes [1880] 1963, p. 225).

Whatever Popper may have thought of economics, it can be demonstrated with his own means: a door is open to extra-scientific values because basic economic theories are not pragmatically falsifiable. Even if they were, ideals are given an opportunity to penetrate the hard core of ideas that is maintained as long as possible. The door is, however, wide open. The fact is, that ideas about a world that is lived in easily become ideals if they relate to action. Welfare theory, for example, which is the result of a formal analysis of 'rational' action, shows us the properties of an idealized timeless system in which the attainment of joint ends is in equilibrium. Of course, the implications can be shown without the introduction of other value judgements than those already contained in the premises, but because it is an – idealized – social decision system, it is a potential ideal. If welfare theory is applied, it functions as an ideal.

However much economists may evoke their purity, they want to change the world. They want to contribute to the solution of urgent *practical* problems. The theories of Quesnay, Smith, Ricardo, Mill, Marx, Walras, Marshall, Pareto, Wicksell, Veblen, Keynes, Schumpeter, Hayek, Tinbergen, Hicks, Friedman and Samuelson contain messages. Perhaps the tame cattle, peacefully grazing in the manner of Kuhn's normal scientists in an area enclosed by definition of Robbins, will succeed in simply enjoying their own digestion. The creative economists, and they are much more numerous than the 'extraordinary' ones according to Kuhn and the 17 listed above, entertain more or less veiled but recognizable ideas about a natural order and a 'meaning' of history, ideas which are not scientifically provable but do help to determine the content of their theories. They try to make the latter acceptable by invoking plausibility.

Sometimes the values of the economists are professed in a wide circle, such as *laissez-faire* in the 19th century or methodological individualism or Pareto-efficiency today. Sometimes, too, the supporters of differing values are irreconcilably opposed, such as the Keynesian interventionists and the monetarist neoliberals, or such as the 'bourgeois' and Marxist economists. However, there is little reason to regard the one ideal as legitimate, formal, indifferent or neutral and the other as a sign of a lack of respect for value-freedom and objectivity. Economic theories cannot be objective. What matters is to explicate the values by self-examination and by unmasking others; to continue the discussion of each relevant aspect, without paying attention to what connoisseurs of the subject matter of economics forbid; to extend empirical research and the study of history; and to abandon the hypocrisy of the so-called value-freedom, about which Weber said untenable things more than 80 years ago.

NOTES

1. Incidentally, neither Smith nor the other classical economists accorded natural liberty an absolute validity. Man adheres to more than one value, and for the sake of 'equilibrium' the one must sometimes give way to the other. For instance, Smith advocated measures for regulating the banking system and admitted: 'Such regulations may, no doubt, be considered as in some respect a violation of natural liberty'. 'Public interest' also proves to be a value for him, for: 'The obligation of building party walls, in order to prevent the communication of fire, is a violation of natural liberty, exactly of the same kind with the regulations of the banking trade which are here proposed' (Smith [1776] 1976b, p. 324).
2. '*Les lois générales dont se composent les sciences politiques et morales ... dérivent de la nature des choses, tout aussi sûrement que les lois du monde physique; on ne les imagine pas, on les trouve; elles gouvernent les gens qui gouvernent les autres et jamais on les viole impunément*' (Say [1803] 1972, pp. 15–16).
3. '*Un Traité d'economie politique se réduira ... à un petit nombre de principes, qu'on n'aura pas même besoin d'appuyer de preuves, parce qu'ils ne seront que l'énoncé de ce que tout le monde saura, arrangé dans un ordre convenable pour en saisir l'ensemble et les rapports*' (Say [1803] 1972, p. 16).
4. Galileo did it in deeds but not in words. Like Newton after him, he adhered to an inductivist methodology, that did not tally with his hypothetico-deductive method.
5. '*Notre démonstration de la libre concurrence en mettant en évidence la question*

132   *Elucidations*

de l'utilité, laisse entièrement de coté la question de justice; car elle se borne à faire sortir une certaine distribution de produits d'une certaine répartition des services, et la queston de cette répartition reste entière' (Walras [1874] 1926, p. 234).

6. *'Per riguardi personali non ho mai detto ... che non accetto in nessun modo il suo modo* [viz. that of Walras] *metafisico di trattare la scienza; ... che non ametto che l'economia pura dimostri come debbono seguire i fatti, mentre a l'inverso; che non accetto di studiare ciò che* deve *essere, ma che in vece studio ciò che è'* (quoted by Jaffé, 1977, p. 380n).

7. *'Nicht darin unterscheiden wir uns ... , dass wir für ein möglichst weitgehende Staatsgewalt schwärmen, sondern darin, dass wir neben der natürlich-technischen auf die psychologischen Ursachen eingehen, dass wir infolge hiervon einen ethischen Entwicklungsprozess der volkswirtschaftlichen Organisationsform annehmen, dass wir an einen Fortschritt glauben, den der konsequente Denker leugnen und unerklärt lassen muss der in der Volkswirtschaft nur eine Naturordnung sieht'* (Schmoller, 1873, p. 65).

8. *'Richtig ist, dass die persönlichen Weltanschauungen auf dem Gebiet unserer Wissenschaften unausgesetzt hineinzuspielen pflegen auch in die wissenschaftliche Argumentation, sie immer wieder trüben, das Gewicht wissenschaftlicher Argumente auch auf dem Gebiet der Ermittlung einfacher kausaler Zusammenhänge von Tatsachen verschieden einschätzen lassen, je nachdem das Resultat die Chance der persönlichen Ideale: die Möglichkeit, etwas Bestimmtes zu wollen, mindert oder steigert. Aber die Herausgeber und Mitarbeiter unserer Zeitschrift werden in dieser Hinsicht sicherlich "nichts Menschliches von sich fern glauben". Aber von diesem Bekenntnis menschlicher Schwäche ist es einen weiten Weg bis zu dem Glauben an eine "ethische" Wissenschaft der Nationalökonomie, welche aus ihrem Stoff ideale oder durch Anwendung allgemeiner ethischer Imperatiove auf ihren Stoff konkrete Normen zu produzieren hätte'* (Weber, 1951, pp. 151–2).

9. Methodological individualism had already been explicitly defended by Joseph Schumpeter and Max Weber.

10. The repercussion of the deeds of the State, intended or unintended are not mentioned. Popper approvingly cites Hayek, his most quoted economist, according to whom economics has never been the product of curiosity but 'of an intense urge to reconstruct a world which gives rise to profound dissatisfaction' (Popper 1957, p. 56), and has been developed chiefly 'as the outcome of the investigation and refutation of successive Utopian proposals (Popper, 1957, p. 58).

11. In a separate note Popper explains this: 'By the "realism" of the choice of our ends I mean that we should choose ends which can be realized within a reasonable span of time, and that we should avoid distant and vague Utopian ideals, unless they determine more immediate aims which are worthy in themselves (Popper [1945] 1966, II, p. 367).

12. *'Der objektive und wertfreie Wissenschaftler ist nicht der ideale Wissenschaftler. Ohne Leidenschaft geht es nicht, und schon gar nicht in der reinen Wissenschaft* (Popper, 1972, p. 114).

13. *'Die Reinheit der reinen Wissenschaft ist ein Ideal, das vermutlich unerreichbar ist, für das aber die Kritik dauernd kämpft und dauernd kämpfen muss'* (Popper, 1972, p. 114).

Bibliography

Albert, H. (1979), 'The Economic Tradition', in Brunner, K. (ed.), *Economics and Social Institutions*, Boston.

Alchian, A.A. (1950), 'Uncertainty, Evolution and Economic Theory', *Journal of Political Economy*.

Archibald, G.C. (1959), 'The State of Economic Science', *The British Journal for the Philosophy of Science*.

Birner, J. (1990), *Strategies and Programmes in Capital Theory*, Dissertation, University of Amsterdam.

Blaug, M. (1980), *The Methodology of Economics*, Cambridge.

Boson, M. (1950), *Léon Walras, fondateur de la politique économique scientifique*, Rennes.

Brentano, L. (1911), 'Über Werturteile in der Volkswirtschaftslehre', *Archiv für Sozialwissenschaft und Sozialpolitik*.

Brunner, K. (1969), '"Assumptions" and the Cognitive Quality of Theories', *Synthese*.

Carnap, R. (1936–7), 'Testability and Meaning', *Philosophy of Science*.

Clark, J.B. (1899), *The Distribution of Wealth*, London.

Cohen, M.R. and Nagel, E. (1963), *An Introduction to Logic and Scientific Method*, London.

Cooper, D.E. (1986), *Metaphor*, Cambridge.

Dampier, W.C. (1971), *A History of Science*, Cambridge.

Dijksterhuis, E.J. (1961), *The Mechanisation of the World Picture*, transl. Dikshoorn, C., Oxford.

Duhem, P. (1976), 'Physical Theory and Experiment', in Harding (1976).

Entrèves, A.P. (1970), *Natural Law*, London.

Feyerabend, P. (1975), *Against Method*, London.

Foss, L. (1971), 'Art as Cognitive: Beyond Scientific Realism', *Philosophy of Science*.

Friedman, M. (1953), *Essays in Positive Economics*, Chicago.

Friedman, M. (ed.) (1956), *Studies in the Quantity Theory of Money*, Chicago.

Friedman, M. and Savage, L.J. (1948), 'The Utility Analysis of Choices Involving Risks', *Journal of Political Economy*.

Frondizi, R. (1971), *What is Value?*, La Salle Ill.

Gäfken, G. (1963), *Theorie der wirtschaftlichen Entscheidung*, Tübingen.

Galbraith, J.K. (1952), *American Capitalism: The Concept of Countervailing Power*, New York.

Gehrig, H. (1914), *Die Begründung des Prinzips der Sozialreform*, Jena.

Goodman, N. (1968), *The Language of Art*, New York.

Gordon, B. (1975), *Economic Analysis Before Adam Smith*, London.

Hacking, I. (1976), *Logic of Statistical Inference*, Cambridge.

Hamminga, L. (1982), *Neoclassical Theory Structure and Theory Development*, Berlin.

Harding, S.G. (ed.) (1976), *Can Theories be Refuted?*, Dordrecht.

Hare, R.M. (1952), *The Language of Morals*, Oxford.

Hayek, F.A. ([1955] 1964), *The Counter-Revolution of Science*, London.

Hume, D. ([1739–40] 1975), *A Treatise of Human Nature*, ed. L. Selby-Biggs, Oxford.

Hutchison, T.W. ([1938] 1965), *The Significance and Basic Postulates of Economic Theories*, New York.

Hutchison, T.W. (1964), *'Positive' Economics and Policy Objectives*, London.

Hutchison, T.W. (1978), *On Revolutions and Progress in Economic Knowledge*, Cambridge.

Jaffé, W. (1977), 'The Normative Bias of the Walrasian Model', *Quarterly Journal of Economics*.

Jeffrey, R.C. (1968), 'Probable Knowledge', in Lakatoa, I. (ed.), *The Problem of Inductive Logic*, Amsterdam.

Kant, I. ([1781] 1956), *Kritik der reinen Vernunft*, Werke, III, Wiesbaden.

Keynes, J.M. ([1921] 1973a), *A Treatise on Probability*, Collected Writings, VIII, London.

Keynes, J.M. ([1933] 1972), *Essays in Biography*, Collected Writings, X, London.

Keynes, J.M. ([1936] 1973), *The General Theory of Employment, Interest and Money*, Collected Writings, VII, London.

Keynes, J.M. (1973b), *The General Theory and After, II*, Collected Writings, XIV, London.

Keynes, J.M. (1983), *Economic Articles and Correspondence*, Collected Writings, XII, London.

Keynes, J.N. ([1880] 1963), *The Scope and Method of Political Economy*, New York.

Klant, J.J. (1984), *The Rules of the Game*, Cambridge.

Klein, L.R. (1951), 'The Life of John Maynard Keynes', *The Journal of Political Economy*.

Klein, L.R. (1971), *An Essay on the Theory of Economic Prediction*, Chicago.

Kuhn, T.S. ([1962] 1970), *The Structure of Scientific Revolutions*, Chicago.

Lakatos, I. (1974), 'Popper on Demarcation and Induction', in Schilpp, P.A. (ed.), *The Philosophy of Karl Popper*, La Salle.

Lakatos, I. (1978), *The Methodology of Scientific Research Programmes*, in Worall, J. and Currie, G. (eds), Cambridge.

Latsis, S.J. (1976a), 'A Research Programme in Economics' in Latsis, S.J. (ed.), *Method and Appraisal in Economics*, Cambridge.

Latsis, S.J. (1976b), 'Situational Determination in Economics', *British Journal for the Philosophy of Science*.

Laudan, L. (1981), *Science and Hypothesis*, Cambridge

Losee, J. ([1972] 1980), *A Historical Introduction to the Philosophy of Science*, Oxford.

MacGrimmon, K.R. and Toda, M. (1969), 'The Experimental Determination of Indifference Curves', *Review of Economic Studies*.

Mach, E. (1906), *Erkenntnis und Irrtum*, Leipzig.

Machlup, F. (1963), In: Papers and Proceedings 75th Annual Meeting AEA, *American Economic Review*.

Machlup, F. (1969), 'Positive and Normative Economics', in Heilbronner, R.L. (ed.), *Economic Means and Social Ends*, Englewood Cliffs.

Malthus, T.R. (1798), *An Essay on the Principal of Population*.

Malthus, T.R. ([1823] 1951), *Principles of Political Economy*, Oxford.

Mannheim, K. ([1928] 1979), *Ideology and Utopia*, London.

Marshall, A. ([1890] 1961), *Principles of Economics*, London.

Marshall, A. ([1925] 1966), 'The Present Position of Economics', in Pigou, A.C. (ed.), *Memorials of Alfred Marshall*, London.

Marx, K. ([1867] 1968), *Das Kapital*, I, Frankfurt.

May, K.O. (1954), 'Intransitivity, Utility and the Aggregation of Preference Patterns', *Econometrica*.

McCloskey, D.N. (1985), *The Rhetoric of Economics*, Wisconsin.

McCloskey, D.N. (1986), 'Economics as a Historical Science', in Parker, W.V. (ed.), *Economic History and the Modern Economist*, Oxford.

Melitz, J. (1953), 'Friedman and Machlup on the Significance of Testing Economic Assumptions', *The Journal of Political Economy*.

Menger, C. (1843), *Untersuchungen über die Methode der Socialwissenschaften, und die Politischen Oekonomie ins besondere*, Leipzig.

Mill, J.S. (1843), *A System of Logic*, London.

Mill, J.S. ([1844] 1974), *Essays on Some Unsettled Questions of Political Economy*, Clifton.

Mill, J.S. ([1848] 1965), *Principles of Political Economy*, Collected Works, II, III, Toronto.

Mirowski, P. and Cook, P. (1990), 'Walras' Economics and Mechanics', in Samuels (1990).

Mises, L. von (1962), *The Ultimate Foundation of Economic Science*, Princeton.

Mitchell, W.C. (1967), *Types of Economic Theory*, J. Dorfman (ed.), New York.

Moggridge, D.E. (1974), *Keynes: Aspects of the Man and his Work*, London.

Myrdal, G. (1958), *Value in Social Theory*, London.

Myrdal, G. (1970), *Objectivity in Social Research*, London.

Nagel, E. (1953), 'Assumptions in Economic Theory', *American Economic Review*.

Nagel, E. (1968), *The Structure of Science*, London.

North, D. ([1691] 1954), *Discourse upon Trade*, in McCulloch, J.R. (ed.), *Early English Tracts* (1856), Cambridge.

Noxon, J. (1975), *Hume's Philosophical Development*, Oxford.

Papandreou, A.G. (1953), 'An Experimental Test of an Axiom in the Theory of Choice', *Econometrica*.

Papandreou, A.G. (1957), *A Test of a Stochastic Theory of Choice*, Berkeley.

Papandreou, A.G. (1958), *Economics as a Science*, Chicago.

Pareto, V. (1906), *Manuel d'économie politique*.

Pareto, V. (1916), *Trattato di sociologica generale*, Florence.

Pigou, A.C. (1912), *Wealth and Welfare*.

Plato (1976), *Protagoras*, transl. C.C.W. Taylor, Oxford.

Popper, K.R. ([1945] 1966), *The Open Society and its Enemies*, London.

Popper, K.R. (1957), *The Poverty of Historicism*, London.

Popper, K.R. (1959), *The Logic of Scientific Discovery*, London.

Popper, K.R. ([1963] 1965), *Conjectures and Refutations*, London.

Popper, K.R. ([1972] 1983), *Objective Knowledge*, Oxford.

Popper, K.R. (1972), 'Die Logik der Sozialwissenschaften' in Adorno, W. (ed.), *Der Positivismusstreit in der Deutschen Soziologie*, Darmstadt.

Popper, K.R. (1975), 'The Rationality of Scientific Revolutions', in Harré, R. (ed.), *Problems of Scientific Revolutions*, Oxford.

Popper, K.R. (1979), *Die beiden Grundprobleme der Erkenntnistheorie*, Tübingen.

Popper, K.R. (1988), *Realism and the Aim of Science*, Bartley III, W.W. (ed.), London.

Quesnay, R. (1958), *La Physiocratie*, Sauvy, A. (ed.), Paris.

Quine, W.V.O. (1976), 'Two Dogmas of Empiricism', in Harding (1976).

Reisman, D. (1976), *Adam Smith's Sociological Economics*, London.

Rescher, N. (1969), *Introduction to Value Theory*, Englewood Cliffs.

Ricardo, D. ([1817] 1970), *On the Principles of Political Economy and Taxation*, Works, I, Cambridge.

Ricardo, D. ([1821] 1973b), *Letters 1819 – June 1821*, Works, VIII, Cambridge.

Ricardo, D. (1973a), *Speeches and Evidences*, Works, V, Cambridge.

Robbins, L. ([1932] 1946), *An Essay on the Nature and Significance of Economic Science*, London.

Robbins, L. (1938), 'Live and Dead Issues in the Methodology of Economics', *Economica*.

Robinson, J. (1948), *The Economics of Imperfect Competition*, London.

Roll, E. (1973), *A History of Economic Thought*, London.

Rotwein, E. (1959), 'The Methodology of Positive Economics', *Quarterly Journal of Economics*.

Runciman, W.G. (1972), *A Critique of Max Weber's Philosophy of Social Science*, Cambridge.

Sahlins, M. (1974), *Stone Age Economics*, London.

Samuels, W.J. (ed.) (1990), *Economics as Discourse*, Boston.

Samuelson, P.A. (1948), *Foundations of Economic Analysis*, Cambridge (Mass.).

Say, J.B. ([1803] 1972), *Traité d'économie politique*, Paris.

Schmoller, G. (1873), 'Sendschreiben', *Jahrbücher für National-ökonomie und Statistik*.

Schmoller, G. (1911), 'Volkswirtschaft, Volkswirtschaftslehre und Methode', *Handwörterbuch der Staatswissenschaft*, VIII, Jena.

Schumpeter, J.A. (1908), *Das Wesen und der Hauptinhalt der theoretischen Nationalökonomie*, Leipzig.

Schumpeter, J.A. (1949), 'Science and Ideology', *American Economic Review*.

Schumpeter, J.A. (1954), *History of Economic Analysis*, London.

Senior, N.W. ([1826] 1966a), *An Introductory Lecture on Political Economy*, in Senior, N.W. *Selected Writings on Economics*, New York.

Senior, N.W. ([1852] 1966b), *Four Introductory Lectures on Political Economy*, in Senior, N.W. *Selected Writings on Economics*, New York.

Simmel, G. ([1900] 1907), *Die Philosophie des Geldes*, Leipzig.

Smith, A. ([1759] 1976a), *The Theory of Moral Sentiments*, Raphael, D.D. and Macfi, A.L. (eds), Oxford.

Smith, A. ([1776] 1976b), *An Inquiry into the Nature and Causes of the Wealth of Nations*, Campbell, R.H., Skinner, A.S. and Todd, W.B. (eds), Oxford.

Smith, A. ([1795] 1980), *Essays on Philosophical Subjects*, Raphael, D.D. and Skinner, A.S. (eds), Oxford.

Sombart, W. (1929), *Die drei Nationalökonomien*, München.

Steuart, J.D. (1767), *An Inquiry into the Principles of Political Oeconomy*.

Stone, R. (1978), *Keynes, Political Arithmetic and Econometrics*, London.

Taylor, P.W. (1961), *Normative Discourse*, Englewood Cliffs.

Theil, H. (1965), *Economic Forecasts and Policy*, Amsterdam.

Tinbergen, J. ([1939] 1968), *Statistical Testing of Business-Cycle Theories*, New York.

Tinbergen, J. (1940), 'On a Method of Statistical Business-Cycle Research: A Reply', *The Economic Journal*.

Tintner, G. (1968), *Methodology of Mathematical Economics and Econometrics*, Chicago.

Toulmin, S. ([1953] 1960), *The Philosophy of Science*, New York.

Toulmin, S. (1972), *Human Understanding*, Oxford.

Verhandlungen der Generalversammlung in Wien 27, 28 und 29 September 1909, *Schriften des Vereins für Sozialpolitik*, Leipzig 1910.

Walker, D.A. (1984), 'Is Walras's Theory of General Equilibrium a Normative Scheme?', *History of Political Economy*.

Wallis, W.A. and Friedman, M. (1942), 'The Empirical Derivation of Indifference Functions', in Lange, O., McIntyre, F. and Yntema, T.

(eds), *Studies in Mathematical Economics and Econometrics'*, Chicago.

Walras, L. ([1874–7] 1926), *Eléments d'économie politique pure*, Paris.

Walras, L. ([1898] 1936), *Etudes d'économie politique appliquée*, Lausanne.

Weber, M. (1951), *Gesammelte Aufsätze zur Wissenschaftsslehre*, Winckelmann, J. (ed.), Tübingen.

Weber, W. and Topitsch, E. (1952), 'Das Wertfreiheitsproblem seit Max Weber', *Zeitschrift für Nationalökonomie*.

Wieser, F. von ([1914] 1924), *Theorie der gesellschaftlichen Wirtschaft*, in *Grundriss der Sozialökonomik*, Tübingen.

Wright, G.H. von (1963), *Norm and Action*, London.

Zarnowitz, V. (1968), 'Prediction and Forecasting', *International Encyclopedia of the Social Sciences*, London.

Index